Stefan Kirchner (Ed.)

Security and Technology in Arctic Governance

Security and Technology in Arctic Governance

edited by

Stefan Kirchner

LIT

This book is printed on acid-free paper.

Bibliographic information published by the Deutsche Nationalbibliothek
The Deutsche Nationalbibliothek lists this publication in the Deutsche Nationalbibliografie; detailed bibliographic data are available in the Internet at http://dnb.dnb.de.
ISBN 978-3-643-91481-1 (pb)
ISBN 978-3-643-96481-6 (PDF)

A catalogue record for this book is available from the British Library.

© LIT VERLAG GmbH & Co. KG Wien,
Zweigniederlassung Zürich 2022
Flössergasse 10
CH-8001 Zürich
Tel. +41 (0) 76-632 84 35
E-Mail: zuerich@lit-verlag.ch   https://www.lit-verlag.ch
Distribution:
In the UK: Global Book Marketing, e-mail: mo@centralbooks.com
In North America: Independent Publishers Group, e-mail: orders@ipgbook.com
In Germany: LIT Verlag Fresnostr. 2, D-48159 Münster
Tel. +49 (0) 2 51-620 32 22, Fax +49 (0) 2 51-922 60 99, e-mail: vertrieb@lit-verlag.de

FOREWORD

In the early days of 1989, when it was still winter in the Arctic but a thaw had begun in international relations between East and West, the government of Finland approached the other Arctic states with the suggestion for a conference on the protection of the natural environment of the Arctic. Later in the same year, government representatives met in the Finnish city of Rovaniemi, the capitol of Finnish Lapland. This marked the starting point for the Arctic Environmental Protection Strategy (AEPS). Over time, this effort at international cooperation would expand. In 1996, the eight Arctic states established the Arctic Council (AC), which to this day remains the most important forum for cross-border cooperation on Arctic governance. Many of the problems we see in the Arctic are shared across the region, including for example climate change and environmental pollution and destruction, colonial legacies, an extremely high rate of suicides in many Arctic communities, and the need for sustainable development and the provision of services and goods to remote communities.

In recent years, Arctic Law and Arctic Governance have emerged as practical realities in the Arctic region and as areas of interest in the Arctic and beyond. Decisions related to the governance of the Arctic are often made far away from the Arctic, for example in national capitols or in international meetings in New York, Geneva or elsewhere. Especially human-made climate change and environmental destruction and pollution impact the Arctic on a great scale and with tremendous speed. Today, the Arctic is warming three times as fast as the rest of the planet. These developments have increased global interest in the Arctic and today more non-Arctic actors want to be involved in decision-making regarding the Arctic, because awareness of the relevance of the Arctic region for the rest of the world is growing. This book is part of an effort to increase awareness of the Arctic, which is home to millions of people, by highlighting a number of selected issues in Arctic governance.

Arctic governance is the attempt to find solutions for problems that are shared across the Arctic region – and in many cases far beyond it. In addition to climate change and environmental problems, these problems include sustainable development and human rights. While the Arctic Council has refrained from discussing hard security issues, questions of security are a concern for Arctic communities. Like security, technology, in particular modern telecommunications technologies, are an integral part of the lives of the people of the Arctic. It is not the intention behind this book to cover all potentially relevant issues concerning security and technology in the Arctic. Instead, it is meant to draw attention to ongoing and emerging challenges in the international governance of this fragile region. The book brings together different voices and approaches. The scholars represented here come from different professional and geographical backgrounds and are at different stages in their respective careers. What unites them is their concern for the Arctic region, the natural environment and for the people who live in the Arctic. The texts collected here are also meant to highlight the diversity of opinions and approaches to Arctic governance. The readers will note, for example, different visions regarding the future of the Arctic, in particular in the context of hydrocarbon extraction in the Arctic. These differing views also reflect the reality of the global debates concerning Arctic governance. It is my hope that this book will inspire debates and discussions and increase awareness of the different approaches to the governance of the Arctic that are possible today.

The Arctic is not an empty space. It is home not only to iconic species, such as Polar Bears, but to a wide range of communities, including indigenous peoples. This book is a modest attempt to draw more attention to their needs and to some of the ongoing challenges that Arctic Governance and Arctic Law will have to address. This requires dialogue, like the ones the authors of this volume had during the preparatory process. It requires cooperation and investments into the future. The essays collected in this small volume is an attempt to keep this spirit alive in the academic community as well.

This book would not have been possible without the financial support of the Arctic Centre of the University of Lapland in Rovaniemi.

Thanks are due especially to the peer reviewers for sharing their time and expertise, to the members of the Arctic Governance research group at the Arctic Centre of the University of Lapland in Rovaniemi, Finland, for the discussions and brainstorming sessions that led to this book, to the team at LIT Verlag and, last but not least, to Laura Ulatowski for enabling the timely publication of this book by patiently and diligently proofreading and formatting the text and creating the index. This book would not exist without her work. All opinions expressed on the following pages are only attributable to the authors of the respective chapters and the usual disclaimers apply.

Stefan Kirchner
20 December 2021

CONTRIBUTORS

Ayonghe Akonwi Nebasifu holds a Master of Arts degree from the University of Lapland in Audiovisual Media. He also holds a Bachelor of Science in Sociology and Anthropology, with a Minor in Journalism and Mass Communication from the University of Buea (Cameroon). He is conducting his doctoral research on the co-management of national parks from the standpoint of anthropological theory. He is a member of the Arctic Governance Research Group at the Arctic Centre of the University of Lapland in Rovaniemi, Finland, coordinating two EU co-funded projects: Sirius Policy Network on Migrant Education and MaxiPAC which aim at facilitating the training and work-life of migrant youths in northern Finland.

Dr. *Federica Cristani* is a Senior Researcher at the Institute of International Relations in Prague, Czech Republic, and a Visiting Senior Researcher at the Arctic Centre of the University of Lapland in Rovaniemi Finland. Earlier she was a Virtual Open Research Laboratory Associate at the Russian, East European, and Eurasian Center of the University of Illinois, USA and Rapporteur in the Comparative COVID19 Project, Institute for New Economic Thinking - Young Scholar Initiative. She earlier worked as a post-doctoral researcher at the World Trade Institute of the University of Berne, Switzerland, and at the University of Verona, Italy, and has been a Visiting Researcher in different universities and research centers in Hungary, Slovakia, Germany, Denmark and the United Kingdom. Her main research interests include international investment law with a focus on sub-regional groups in Europe and cybersecurity.

Medy Dervovic holds an LL.M in Polar Law from the University of Akureyri, Iceland. His main interests are Arctic governance, the law of the sea, public international law, environmental law, and human rights. In 2021-2022, he is an ERASMUS+ trainee at the Arctic Centre of the University of Lapland in Rovaniemi, Fin

Katharina Heinrich (M.A. Polar Law) is a junior researcher in the Arctic Governance Research Group at the Arctic Centre, University of Lapland in Rovaniemi, Finland. With a background in Arctic and Antarctic Law and Policy, as well as Coastal and Marine Management, her research interests cover a wide field. Thereby, her research mainly focuses on the Law of the Sea, Marine Biodiversity Conservation and Management, and how these processes are affected by climate change impacts, especially in the Polar Regions.

Prof. Dr. *Stefan Kirchner* is Research Professor of Arctic Law and heads the Arctic Governance Research Group at the Arctic Centre of the University of Lapland in Rovaniemi, Finland. He is admitted to the bar in Germany and has taught at universities in Finland, Germany, Greenland, Italy, Lithuania and Ukraine. Prof. Kirchner is a member of the leadership team of the International Disaster, Emergency and Law Network co-chair of the Space Law Interest Group of the American Society of International Law. His work on this volume is undertaken in his private capacity and does not reflect the views of any institutions or organizations he is affiliated with.

Mirva Salminen is working as a researcher in the LEXSECURE project (funded by the Academy of Finland) at the Faculty of Law of the University of Lapland. The project examines the legal basis of supranational supply chains and how the availability of critical commodities such as healthcare products can be secured in global crises. At the Arctic Centre, Mirva is carrying out research on digitalization and cybersecurity in the Arctic – the topic on which she has also written her doctoral thesis (Political Science) to the Faculty of Social Sciences at the University of Lapland. Prior to joining the University of Lapland, she worked in research and expert positions in the field of cybersecurity in both public and private sectors.

Álvaro Augusto Sanabria-Rangel is a PhD researcher at the University of Lapland Faculty of Law, and holds a master's degree in Political Sciences with the major subject International Law within the

Degree Program in International Human Rights Law from Åbo Akademi University. He is also one of the founding members of Miilza Project Ry, an NGO based in Helsinki whose aim is to promote human rights and youth rights within marginalized communities. His main research topics are international human rights law, international law, victim's rights and environmental law.

Pavel Tkach (M.A. Polar Law) is a junior researcher in the Arctic Migration team of the Arctic Governance Research Group at the Arctic Centre, University of Lapland. With a background in Arctic Law and Policy, as well as Russian law and EU law, his research interests cover various fields of law. His research mainly focuses on Migration law, Commercial law, Intellectual Property law, and how the features of the Arctic regions affect the development of mentioned fields of law.

Yue Wang is a Doctoral Researcher in International Relations at Tampere University in Finland, and a Visiting Researcher at the Arctic Centre, University of Lapland. He graduated *cum laude* with a master's degree in International Relations from the University of Groningen in the Netherlands and holds a bachelor's degree with *Honors* in History from a Chinese university. His main research interests are international politics in the Arctic (especially the role of non-Arctic actors), unintended consequences of international cooperation, and Sino-EU relations.

Liling Xu is a PhD researcher at Royal Holloway, University of London, and holds a master's degree in International Relations at Tongji University, China. Liling Xu's main research interests are China's policies and practices in the Arctic, and critical geopolitics. Her PhD research project focuses on China's geopolitical imaginations of the Arctic, which is mainly situated in critical geopolitics and informed by an array of scholarship including feminist geopolitics, emotional geopolitics, tourism geopolitics, etc.

TABLE OF CONTENTS

INTRODUCTION 1

Mirva Salminen

VESSEL-SOURCE POLLUTION IN THE ARCTIC OCEAN: COMPETING INTERESTS OF FLAG STATES AND COASTAL STATES 13

Stefan Kirchner & Katharina Heinrich

LEGALITY OF FOREIGN MILITARY ACTIVITIES IN THE EXCLUSIVE ECONOMIC ZONE: LESSONS FROM THE 2020 BERING SEA INCIDENT 33

Medy Dervovic & Pavel Tkach

ASSESSING CHINA'S SECURITIZATION OF ARCTIC CLIMATE CHANGE AND ENERGY 57

Yue Wang & Liling Xu

ASSESSING THE IMPACT OF DISASTERS ON TECHNOLOGY TRANSFER UNDER INTERNATIONAL ECONOMIC LAW: THE CASE OF SPACE-BASED TECHNOLOGIES 115

Federica Cristani

SPACE OPERATIONS AND THE NATURAL ENVIRONMENT OF THE ARCTIC 139

Stefan Kirchner & Alvaro Sanabria-Rangel

VIII

THE EUROPEAN UNION'S PROPOSAL FOR A BAN ON ARCTIC OIL, GAS AND COAL EXPLORATION, EXTRACTION AND TRADE 165

Stefan Kirchner

CONCLUSIONS AND OUTLOOK 173

Ayonghe Akonwi Nebasifu

EPILOGUE 185

Stefan Kirchner

INDEX 187

INTRODUCTION
Mirva Salminen

Setting the scene

This edited volume on Arctic governance, security and technology is the end result of an idea that emerged within the Arctic Governance research group of the Arctic Centre, University of Lapland at the turn of the year 2021.

Many of the scholars in the group have a background in international law, for which reason the perspective to governance lies heavily on law throughout the volume, although the intention has not been to de-emphasise the political, economic, social or cultural sides of governance. In addition, all of the articles have their own, independent perspectives to both security and technology. While it can be presumed that the reader of this volume is somewhat familiar with the complexities of the multi-layered Arctic governance, the two other concepts may seem less problematic. Yet, it is their complexities that I will focus on in this introduction.

Before turning to the introduction's structure, one further notion is in place. The Arctic in these articles is not univocal signifier either but refers *inter alia* to the Arctic Ocean; the Arctic states; the Arctic people(s); the Arctic lands, including everything under and above the ground; the Arctic nature and environment; dependencies on, across, and of the Arctic; mental images hold of the Arctic; as well as a target of policies, regulation, and power projection. This fact in itself reminds the reader of the manifoldness of the Arctic. None of the authors has indigenous background, which would have undoubtedly diversified the understanding of the Arctic even more.

The structure of this introduction is the following: I will first spend some time on defining both security and technology. Second, I will briefly introduce the six articles of this volume.

Defining the core concepts
Security
As mentioned, all of the six articles of this volume rely on different understandings of technology, discuss different technologies and knowledges, and also entail different understandings of security. I will begin the unwinding of these conceptualisations from security. David A. Baldwin noted towards the turn on the millennium that most attempts to redefine security "are more concerned with redefining the policy agendas of nation-states than with the concept of security itself. Often, [these attempts take] the form of proposals for giving high priority to such issues as human rights, economics, the environment, [...] or social injustice, in addition to the traditional concern with security from external military threats. Such proposals are usually buttressed with a mixture of normative arguments about which values of which people or groups of people should be protected, and empirical arguments as to the nature and magnitude of threats to those values." (Baldwin, 1997, p. 5.) The aforementioned holds true for this volume as well, even if the attempt has been to redefine neither security nor technology but to study their interlinkages in the Arctic.

According to Baldwin (1997, p. 12), the conceptual discussion concerning security "begins with specifications for defining security as a policy objective and proceeds to specifications for defining policies for pursuing that objective". He is here referring to Arnold Wolfers's (1952, pp. 483; 485) formulation of national security "to designate an objective of policy distinguishable from others" that "suggests protection through power" understood as "ability to control the actions of others". Furthermore, "[t]he demand for a policy of national security is primarily normative in character. It is supposed to indicate what the policy of a nation should be in order to be either expedient [...] or moral", and hence always embeds value judgements (Wolfers, 1952, pp. 483–484). The problem with security is that it "covers a range of goals so wide that highly divergent policies can be interpreted as policies of security" (Wolfers, p. 484) for which reason the conceptual discussion is of great importance.

Wolfers (1952, pp. 484, 493) remarks that security always "points to some degree of protection of values previously acquired". In addition, "[s]ecurity [itself] is a value, [...] of which a nation can have more or less and which it can aspire to have in greater or lesser measure" (Wolfers, 1952, pp. 484, 493). "In an objective sense, [security] measures the absence of threats to acquired values, [and] in a subjective sense, the absence of fear that such values will be attacked" (Wolfers, 1952, p. 485). Thus, security "is nothing but the absence of the evil of insecurity, a negative value so to speak" (Wolfers, 1952, p. 488). Because "every increment of security must be paid by additional sacrifices of other values" (Wolfers, 1952, p. 494), "absolute security is unattainable" (Baldwin, 1997, p. 15). "As a consequence, nations will be inclined to minimize [security] efforts, keeping them at the lowest level which will provide them with what they consider adequate protection" (Wolfers, 1952, p. 488). Furthermore, "security policies [...] based on the accumulation of power have a way of defeating themselves if the target level is set too high" and lead to the so-called security dilemma[1] (Wolfers, 1952, p. 494). Baldwin (1997, p. 13) rebalances Wolfers's accounts by highlighting the preservation of acquired values instead of underlining threats, which widens the conceptualisation of security to sources of insecurity that are unintentional, such as pandemics or natural hazards. Baldwin continues his specification of the concept of security by formulating a set of questions that ought to be answered by any account of security. First two, that is, *security for whom* and *security for*

---

[1] Security dilemma is a concept described by John Herz (1950, p. 157) for men, groups, and their leaders living in an anarchic society: "Groups or individuals living in such a constellation must be, and usually are, concerned about their security from being attacked, subjected, dominated, or annihilated by other groups and individuals. Striving to attain security from such attack, they are driven to acquire more and more power in order to escape the impact of the power of others. This, in turn, renders the others more insecure and compels them to prepare for the worst. Since none can ever feel entirely secure in such a world of competing units, power competition ensues, and the vicious circle of security and power accumulation is on." The concept has been refined ever since, but its basic dynamic remains the same.

which values, concern the objective of security (Baldwin, 1997, pp. 13–14). As the chapters of this volume also indicate, the referent objects of security can be manifold, but a failure to indicate the protected values weakens any security policy, whether formal or informal. With regard to the policies to advance or sustain security, Baldwin (1997, pp. 14–17) provides five additional questions to consider: *How much security? From what threats? By what means? At what cost?* And *in what time period?* Concerning the last question, he notes that "[t]he most rational policies for security in the long run may differ greatly from those for security in the short run" (Baldwin, 1997, p. 17), which implicates a need to accommodate between these two timeframes. In the Arctic, this accommodation need becomes highlighted by climate change and its consequences to all aspects of security.

While Baldwin's questions remain an excellent framework for conducting and, consequentially, reading studies on security, Wolfers's notions about security have been supplemented by later research. A pivotal addition has been a remark about positive security, which, for example, Gunhild Hoogensen et al. (2009, p. 3) have specified in the following manner: "Security is achieved when individuals and/or multiple actors have the freedom to identify risks and threats to their well-being and values (negative security), the opportunity to articulate these threats to other actors, and the capacity to determine ways to end, mitigate or adapt to those risks and threats either individually or in concert with other actors (positive security)". This formulation, first, shifts the focus from high-politics and national security to low-politics and 'everyday', 'human' or 'vernacular' securities. Thus, it provides other-than-only-the-state answer to the whose security question, which has implications for answering to the consequent questions. Second, alongside freedom from threats and fear, it emphasises freedom to act according to one's own premises (e.g. Hoogensen Gjørv, 2012, p. 836) hence extending security beyond formal security policies and, especially, beyond the notion of protection

through power/control. Security "is a good which provides the foundation to allow us to pursue our needs and interests and enjoy a full life" (Hoogensen Gjørv, 2012, p. 836).
Security is hence to be understood as a continuous process (Hoogensen et al., 2009, p. 2) to which its objective and subjective, negative and positive aspects contribute in a dialogue and in a mutually constitutive way. Next, I will turn to the second central concept of this volume, technology.

Technology
Like security, technology can be defined in a number of ways – some rather narrow, while others close to all-encompassing. Some forty years ago, Friedrich Rapp (1981, p. 1) noted how "technology [directly or indirectly] influences all areas of individual and social life". "While there is a wide-spread tendency to accept unreflectively the accomplishments and conveniences of technology, its negative consequences are more likely to lead to reflection and criticism" (Rapp, 1981, pp. 1–2). The chapters of this volume similarly address both the benefits and drawbacks of technology, even if their legal focus tends to emphasise the need to regulate technologies due to their negative effects.
Rapp does not provide similar questions to those of Baldwin to answer to in the conceptualisation of technology, but gives some aspects to concentrate on while also addressing the kinds of knowledge associated. "When discussing the *meaning* of technological actions or the *criteria* of technical decision-making, we cannot avoid a 'humanistic' reflection on values. [However, if] the issue is one of determining the range of technically possible *solutions* for a given problem or of predicting the physical *consequences* of any particular technological decision, it is only the scientist or engineer who can competently inform us." (Rapp, 1981, p. 3, italics original.) Different emphasis given to different aspects of technology at different times in different contexts have then led to a number of varying definitions of technology.

In a narrow sense, 'technology' can be understood as 'technique', that is, a certain procedure such as a learnable skill. In a broader sense, it entails a collection of procedures and "all objects connected with such procedures" that "are *used* in technological processes [...] or are *produced* as the result of such processes [...]". (Rapp, 1981, p. 31, italics original.) The distinction between 'technique' and 'technology' has also been made by emphasising that "[t]he cognates of 'technology' generally refer to the science of or discourses about the practical, material arts, while cognates of 'technique' are applied to the actual processes and methods of these activities" (Mitcham and Schatzberg, 2009, p. 27). Thus, "[u]pon closer scrutiny, from the perspective of technology as efficient, goal-oriented activity, two [further] aspects emerge: technology as procedural *knowledge* and as *actual execution*". When the complexity of technology increases, "prior theoretical knowledge becomes the indispensable condition for successful practical action", which approximates technology with science. (Rapp, 1981, p. 32, italics original.)

In addition, "[c]omplex technological activities are always *social action processes*, involving [...] groups of participants" and hence embedding in social contexts and calling for specialisation and coordination (Rapp, 1981, p. 32, italics original). Finally, if one focuses "on the material substratum upon which the respective actions are carried out, then technology is seen to be the result of purposefully caused *natural processes*. Such processes are artificial inasmuch as technological objects and processes do not occur in nature untouched by man [, but] they are natural [...] inasmuch as they are subject to the natural laws of the material world." (Rapp, 1981, p. 33, italics original.)

Technology has thus been defined, for instance, as the "transformation of nature through the intellect", which entails working on both organic and inorganic nature, as well as on one's own intellectual and psychological nature, according to one's goals and "in proportion to [one's] understanding of natural laws" (Beck, 1969, pp. 29–31; see Rapp, 1981, pp. 33–34). Resembling some aspects of Wolfers' definition of security, technology in the subjective sense has been defined "as the art of the right way to an end [...] and in the objective sense [as] the refined totality of procedures and instruments within a defined specified area of human activity". The most reasonable way, calculated by the unit of success, is the one requiring least expenditure as it also provides maximum success, calculated by the unit of expenditure. (von Gottl-Ottlilienfeld, 1914, pp. 207, 211; see Rapp, 1981, p. 34.) Quite differently, technology has also been defined by its content and "the particular processes involved in innovation" such as "organisational, political, economic and cultural [...] which pattern the design and implementation of technology" (Williams and Edge, 1996, pp. 865–866). Technology hence "does not develop according to an inner technological logic but is instead a social product" that advances through (policy) choices between different technical options (Williams and Edge, 1996, p. 866).

All these definitions have common features. First, "technological action is always tied to ideological presuppositions" such as worldviews and corresponding technical knowledges as well as a motivation "to channel technological potential in a certain direction" (Rapp, 1981, p. 25). Second, the "concrete execution of the technological process depends on certain material prerequisites such as raw materials and tools along with appropriate forms of organization". Third, alongside the immediate results "we must account for the secondary impacts of technological activity on man himself and on the environment". (Rapp, 1981, p. 25) For more sophisticated definitions of technology, Carl Mitcham and Eric Schatzberg (2009, pp. 58–59) suggest considering the following ten questions:

- Does technology have an inner or essential distinguishing feature?
- If technology has essential and/or necessary feature(s), how may such be distinguished from accidental and/or contingent features?
- What is the relation between technology and nature?
- What is the relation between technology and human action?
- Is technology one or many, that is, a unity or plurality?

- What, if any, are the parts of / divisions within technology?
- Is there historical continuity in the development of technology?
- What is the relation between technology and science?
- What is the relation between technology and engineering?
- What is the relation between technology and other aspects of human life, such as culture, language, religion, art, society, politics, economics, etcetera?

While the articles included in this volume do not systematically address the aforementioned questions concerning security and technology, the reader may keep them in mind and/or return to them when going through the different accounts of security and technology in Arctic governance briefly introduced next.

Introducing the articles of this volume
In the first chapter, Stefan Kirchner and Katharina Heinrich provide an overview of the binding legal tools available for controlling vessel-source pollution in the Arctic Ocean. Operating in the field of marine environmental law, they consider the interests and obligations of coastal states and flag states in international governance. Their main concern is environmental security, but also the security of individuals and communities whose lives and livelihoods the prospective cruise ship operations in the Arctic will affect. Therefore, they ask which binding legal norms exist that can be utilised to protect the Arctic marine environment and the health and wellbeing of local residents. International law of the sea provides the regulatory framework for the Arctic Ocean, which has been supplemented with other regulation, for example, treaties negotiated under the umbrella of the Arctic Council. However, the overall legal picture of marine environmental protection in the Arctic remains spotty. For this reason, additional regulation may be required to address water and air pollution, as well as gaps in seafarer training.

The second chapter considers two mainstream security settings, namely, military security and economic security in the Exclusive Economic Zones (EEZ) of the Arctic Ocean. Medy Dervovic and Pavel Tkach are interested in the Russian military manoeuvres in the Bering Sea under the Ocean Shield 2020 exercise; particularly, an incident between US-flagged fishing vessels and Russian military vessels and aircraft in the border area of the Russian and the US EEZ. Their main question is to what extent the Russian military exercise in the Bering Sea was or could be considered lawful according to the international law of the sea, which considers the peaceful use of the seas a fundamental principle. As the EEZ legal regime leaves unclear the treatment of foreign military activities, circumstantial elements related to *inter alia* prior notification through appropriate communication channels and the establishment of maritime exclusion/safety zones influence the evaluation of such activities' legality in practice. Yue Wang and Liling Xu continue on the line of national security and in their chapter examine China's role in the contemporary security setting in the Arctic. They first point out the duality of China's Arctic policy which emphasises peace and security while also embeds a clear interest, for example, in resources development and new shipping routes. China incorporated the polar regions into its National Security Law in 2015, which lays the legal foundation for protecting its national interests and rights in the Arctic. Thus, second, the authors explore the role that China plays in the securitisation of the Arctic and whether China takes exceptional measures towards such securitisation. Their exploration is carried out by looking into how securitising actors and functional actors construct existential threats in the Arctic to security referent objects in China. The main argument is that China's securitisation of the Arctic has not been on its national security agenda, while securitising moves take place with regard to climate change, energy, and navigation affairs. Moreover, the 'ambiguity' of China's discourses links environmental and economic security to national security and to its tendency to portray these issues as questions of development.

In the fourth chapter, Federica Cristani investigates the economic consequences of natural disasters for affected states regarding technology transfer in particular and using space-based technology transfer in the Arctic as a case-study. Space-based technology has become an important element in risk reduction strategies and proven to be particularly useful in the Arctic, but do disasters impact technology transfer processes and which (international) instruments then come into play? After defining what 'disaster' entails in international law and what 'technology transfer' is, the chapter provides a mapping of technology transfer provisions in international disaster law instruments, international economic law, and space law. While the international regulatory framework of technology transfer in the context of disasters is quite fragmented, a practical peculiarity in the Arctic is wide cooperation in space-based technology transfer which takes place between all relevant stakeholders.

Stefan Kirchner and Alvaro Sanabria-Rangel continue on the topic of space technologies and in their chapter consider the effect of space operations on environmental security and both personal and community security in the Arctic. The article's starting point is the dependency of modern life on space operations in terms of, for example, communication and navigation. Such operations, however, create negative environmental impacts. In the past decades, public international law has undergone fragmentation, which creates a risk of legal actors overlooking connections between the different fields of law and missing the big picture of governing, for example, space technologies. By emphasizing human rights in environmental protection and by focusing on the case law of the European and the Inter-American Court of Human Rights, the authors aim to show that coherence in public international law is essential and that human rights can provide the interlinking factor. Their main argument is that by honouring the duty to respect international human rights law states can expand space law without a need for formal changes to space law treaties. Future space law, however, should include environmental and human rights obligations *expressis verbis*.

The final chapter discusses oil, gas and coal exploration, extraction and trade in the Arctic. Stefan Kirchner focuses on the European Union's new Arctic policy (published on October 13, 2021) and, in particular, on its commitment to ensuring that oil, coal and gas stay in the ground. Such a commitment is to be read in the light of environmental security and the Union's efforts to combat climate change. The EU has two goals: the creation of an internationally binding legal obligation that outlaws Arctic hydrocarbon development and a legally binding obligation to refrain from purchasing such hydrocarbons. As the former will require the consent of the Arctic states, it currently seems elusive given the relevance of hydrocarbon extraction for some of the Arctic national economies. The latter could be utilised immediately if the EU Member States refrained from purchasing oil and gas from the Arctic. The Union's position on hydrocarbon extraction has changed over the years and the practical impact of this commitment and how it relates to EU-level and international legal obligations in the long run remains to be seen.

This contribution is a result of the research project LEXSECURE Law for Secure Supply: Internalizing the Crisis Exceptions funded by the Academy of Finland (2020–2023), decision: 338644.

References
1. Baldwin, David A. (1997) The Concept of Security. *Review of International Studies* 23(1), pp. 5–26. https://doi.org/10.1017/S0260210597000053.
2. Beck, Heinrich (1969) *Philosophie der Technik - Perspektiven zu Technik-Menschheit-Zukunft.* Trier: Spee Verlag.
3. von Gottl-Ottlilienfeld, Friedrich (1914) Wirtschaft und Technik (Grundriß der Sozialokönomik, section 5). Tübingen: J.C.B. Mohr.
4. Herz, John H. (1950) Idealist Internationalism and the Security Dilemma. *World Politics* 2(2), pp. 157–180. https://www.jstor.org/stable/2009187.

5. Hoogensen, Gunhild, Bazely, Dawn, Christensen, Julia, Tanentzap, Andrew, & Bojko, Evgeny (2009) Human Security in the Arctic – Yes, it is Relevant! *Journal of Human Security* 5(2), pp. 1–10. https://doi.org/10.3316/JHS0502001.
6. Hoogensen Gjørv, Gunhild (2012) Security by any other name: negative security, positive security, and a multi-actor security approach. *Review of International Studies* 38(4), pp. 835–859. https://doi.org/10.1017/S0260210511000751.
7. Mitcham, Carl, & Schatzberg, Eric (2009) Defining Technology and Engineering Sciences. In: Meijers, Anthonie (Ed.) *Philosophy of Technology and Engineering Sciences*. Volume 9 in Gabbay, Dov, Thagard, Paul, & Woods, John (Eds.) Handbook of the Philosophy Science. Burlington (MA): Elsevier, pp. 27–63.
8. Rapp, Friedrich (1981) *Analytical Philosophy of Technology*. English translation by Stanley R. Carpenter and Theodor Lagenbruch. Volume 63 in Cohen, Robert S., & Wartofsky, Marx W. (Eds.) Boston Studies in Philosophy of Science. Dordrecth: D. Reidel.
9. Williams, Robin, & Edge, David (1996) The social shaping of technology. *Research Policy* 25(6), pp. 865–899. https://doi.org/10.1016/0048-7333(96)00885-2.
10. Wolfers, Arnold (1952) "National Security" as an Ambiguous Symbol. *Political Science Quarterly* 67(4), pp. 481–502. https://www.jstor.org/stable/21451

VESSEL-SOURCE POLLUTION IN THE ARCTIC OCEAN: COMPETING INTERESTS OF FLAG STATES AND COASTAL STATES

Stefan Kirchner & Katharina Heinrich

Abstract: With the opening of the Arctic Ocean, as a result of climate change impacts, an increased interest in the use of Arctic marine spaces, through maritime activities, including shipping activities, can be seen. As these activities are expected to increase in the future of a changing Arctic, new opportunities but also challenges prevail for the governance framework of the region. Vessel-sourced pollution, amongst others, presents a main risk for Arctic biodiversity and Arctic communities, which are often relying to a large extent on the marine environment. Thus, the chapter explores the past, current and future aspects of international governance of the Arctic Ocean considering the different interests of flag and coastal states.
Key words: Arctic shipping, marine pollution, GHG emissions, IMO

Introduction

The Arctic Ocean is gaining global attention, particularly in connection with the use of Arctic waters for maritime transport. In this chapter, the reader will be introduced to general considerations concerning the international governance of the Arctic Ocean with regard to the different interests of flag states, i.e., states where ships are registered that the flag of which they fly, and coastal states. To this end, existing academic literature from the Arctic and beyond will be analysed and placed in the context of current developments.
Marine environmental law is significantly influenced by international law (Kahl & Gärditz, 2019, p. 458) and tackling vessel-source pollution requires legal action from both flag states and coastal states (Ringbom, 2015, p. 105). While coastal states have the legal capacity to protect the marine environment in their internal waters (to which Canada also counts the waters of the NWP), the territorial sea and,

to some degree as permitted by Article 56 para. 1 lit. (a) of the United Nations Convention on the Law of the Sea (UNCLOS), the Exclusive Economic Zone (EEZ), a competence that can be expanded for ice-covered areas of the EEZ according to Article 234 UNCLOS, the flag state is entirely responsible for vessel-source pollution in areas beyond national jurisdiction, that is, in particular in the high seas portion of the Central Arctic Ocean (CAO). Despite the geographical distance of the CAO to the coast, the fragility of the marine environment of the Arctic Ocean requires a holistic approach to the protection of the entire Arctic Ocean biosphere. In the following, existing international legal norms will be examined through an analysis of legal documents and academic literature in order to show which hard, i.e., binding, legal norms exist that might be utilized to protect the Arctic marine environment and the health of local residents. In this context, the emphasis will shift to the role of the coastal states beyond the aforementioned regulatory opportunities afforded by UNCLOS. In addition, light will be shed on the role of industry standards before an attempt will be made to look into the potential future of cruise ship operations in the Arctic and their international legal regulation. The focus of this chapter will be on the protection of the environment. The reason for this approach is found in the dependence of everybody in the Arctic on nature. Through the protection of the natural environment it is possible to make substantial contributions to the protection of human health and the cultural and other rights of the people who live along the coasts.

A "new" Ocean
The Arctic Ocean is becoming largely ice-free for the first time in human history. This raises the question as to how this "new ocean" (a frequently used term, see e.g. Koivurova et al., 2019; Koivurova et al., 2020; and the title of an earlier project by this author, see Kirchner & Pääkkölä, 2019) and its uses can be regulated. Unlike in the case of Antarctica, the Arctic, which is home to millions of people and where nation states exercise sovereignty and sovereign

rights, there is no single Arctic treaty. This, however, does not mean, that the Arctic is lawless. The opposite is actually the case.

International Law for the Arctic Ocean
The International Law of the Seas as the Fundamental Legal Framework for the Arctic Ocean
In the 2008 Ilulissat Declaration, the coastal states of the Arctic Ocean agreed that the international law of the sea provides the regulatory framework for the Arctic Ocean. While UNCLOS forms the fundament and general framework for the international law of the sea, customary international law and other international treaties and regulations created on the basis of these treaties are additional elements of the totality of international rules that regulate international ship operations. In the case of Arctic ship operations, the International Convention for the Safety of Life at Sea (SOLAS) and the International Convention for the Prevention of Pollution from Ships (MARPOL) provide significant rules that help to provide safety to vessels and the people who work on them and to protect the ocean environment. On the basis of both SOLAS and MARPOL, the Polar Code has been adopted through the International Maritime Organization (IMO), an international organization that has been given a specific legal status in the international law of the sea, as a binding set of norms that aim to enhance safety and environmental protection in the Arctic and Southern Oceans, taking into account dangers that are specific to polar waters.

Air Pollution and Climate Change
While oil pollution from ships would be disastrous for the marine environment in the Arctic (see Wadhams, 2017, p. 99), water pollution is not the only threat that emanates from increased maritime traffic in the region. An important form of pollution from ships is air pollution that is not the result of an accident but a consequence of the operation of vessels. Under MARPOL, regional Emission Control Areas (ECAs), for example in the Baltic Sea (cf. Section 3 of

Regulation 14 in Annex VI to MARPOL), have been expanded, including Sulphur Emission Control Areas (SECAs), where only ship diesel with reduced sulphur content may be used. Since the beginning of 2020, these regional requirements have been taken to the global level through Regulation 14, Section 1.3, of Annex VI to MARPOL. Prior to 2020, ship owners faced two compliance options, either to install scrubbers, functioning somewhat similar to catalyzers in cars, or to switch to low-sulphur content fuels. The latter choice has been the preferred course of action for most ship operators to comply with the global sulphur limit. Although technically only referring to sulphur contents in ship fuels, this measure already goes a way towards reducing the air pollution from ships - but this improvement is happening on a very low level. Air pollution from ships continues to be a problem not only with regard to the health effects of air pollution but also in the context of climate change.

Regulations towards the reduction of GHG emissions from ships
The third Greenhouse Gas (GHG) Study (2014) of the IMO suggests that GHG emissions from ships account for about 2.4% of the global share between 2007 and 2012. Furthermore, it is assessed that the increase of emitted CO_2, which is the most important GHG emitted from ships, lies between 50% and 250% from 2012 to 2050 based on the business as usual scenario (MEPC 67/INF.3). As such, the study shows that GHG emissions are likely to increase in the future with the expanding demand of maritime transportation. Also, in the Arctic, an increase of shipping activities related to maritime transportation might be seen with the opening of the region through climate change impacts. However, to date the increase in Arctic maritime activities is still largely characterized by the operation of fishing vessels (PAME, 2020). Even though, the reduction of GHG emissions has already been acknowledged internationally through its inclusion in international environmental legislation instruments, beginning with the 1992 United Nations Framework Convention on Climate

Change (UNFCCC), the above outlined developments in the international shipping industry show the continued need for effectively implemented measures to reduce GHG emissions on a global level. The first GHG study conducted in 2000 by the Marine Environment Protection Committee (MEPC) of the IMO is, amongst others, based on the mandate of the IMO to reduce GHG emissions from international shipping, which has been transferred to the organisation by the 1997 Kyoto Protocol to the UNFCCC (1997). This is laid out in its Article 2 (2), according to which states listed in Annex I, are obliged to limit or reduce GHG emissions not controlled by the Montreal Protocol through the IMO. The Paris Agreement under the UNFCCC adopted in 2015, which substitutes the Kyoto Protocol, on the other hand, does not refer to the IMO in specific. However, the IMO has used and continues to use its mandate to adopt and facilitate the highest practicable standards in relation to maritime safety, efficiency of navigation and the prevention and control of marine pollutions from ships, which has been officially transferred by the Kyoto Protocol (Chircop, 2019, p. 488; and IMO Convention, 1948, Art.1(a)). On this basis, the IMO established, since the late 90s, several regulatory measures to reduce GHG emissions. A breakthrough in the regulation of GHG emissions from shipping through the IMO was marked by the entry into force of the latest revised Annex VI to MARPOL 73/78 in 2010 (Shi and Gullett, 2018, p. 137). As such, Annex VI regulates emissions of ozone-depleting substances in addition to setting out technical and operational efficiency measures, in particular the mandatory Energy Efficiency Design Index (EEDI) as a requirement for new ships and the Ship Energy Efficiency Management Plan (SEEMP) for example (Chircop, 2019, p. 488-489).

However, the establishment of specific regulatory measures to reduce GHG emissions from shipping has proven to be challenging. As a result, GHG emissions are, to date, only partially regulated under the IMO and discussions concerning limits to GHG emissions by ships are still underway. These continued discussions are, in addition to that, rooted in the conflicting principles enshrined in international environmental law regulations and regulations of international fora, such as the IMO.

An accepted guiding principle in international standards and rules regarding climate change is the "common but differentiated responsibilities and respective capabilities principle" (CBDR-RC), which is enshrined in the UNFCCC and inherited by the Kyoto Protocol and the Paris Agreement (see for example: UNFCCC Art. 3.1, 3.2, and 4; Kyoto Protocol Art. 10; and Paris Agreement preamble, Art. 2.2, 4.3 et seq.). The principle thereby refers to each country's obligation to take responsibility for climate change impacts resulting from anthropogenic activities. Yet, according to the principle, developed countries should bear the primary responsibility as they are the source of the largest historic and current GHG emissions (Chen, 2021). The Kyoto Protocol even provides quantified reduction targets of GHG emissions for each specific developed country and additionally introduces flexible mechanisms and funds, which aim to support developed countries to achieve their commitments. In addition to that, technology transfer and financial assistance shall be provided to support developing countries to achieve the global reduction of GHG emissions (Chen, 2021). The Paris Agreement, on the other hand, provides a more flexible interpretation of the principle as it creates obligations for state parties in a more dynamic manner. As such, it establishes mandatory obligations for all countries but provides plans that are adjusted to national circumstances irrespective the industry, geography or economy (Chircop, 2019, p. 483). MARPOL and IMO standards to restrict GHG emissions from international shipping however are based on the principle of non-discrimination and equal treatment, as well as the "No More Favourable Treatment" (NMFT) principle, according to which the same regulatory measures apply to all ships irrespective their flag, also known as "flag state neutrality" (Chen, 2021).

The presence of these two conflicting principles creates discords between developed and developing states regarding measures to reduce GHG emissions from international shipping activities. As such, developed countries argue that regulations of GHG emissions from international shipping shall be applicable to all ships according to the NMFT principle. Developing states on the other hand support the application of the CBDR principle and insist that any GHG-emitted regulations that are adopted by the IMO should be applicable to Annex I parties, set out in the UNFCCC and the Kyoto Protocol (Chen, 2021). Thus, none of the IMO international treaty instruments currently apply selectively to ships according to their flag.

As a result, the Initial IMO Strategy on Reduction of GHG Emissions from Ships (2018) aims to find a balance between these conflicting principles and incorporates both, the CBDR principle, as well as the principle of non-discrimination and the NMFT principle (see: IMO Initial Strategy, 2018, Annex 3.2). In consequence, the IMO faces regulatory challenges in achieving a balance between the interests of developed and developing states. The difficulty becomes especially evident when considering the outcomes by only implementing one of the principles. As Shi and Gullet (2018) outlined, choosing to not include the CBDR principle can lead to disproportionate burdens that will be, as a result, imposed on developing states, through the flag of convenience practice for example. However, implementing the NMFT contrarily, can lead to inefficiency of GHG regulations, as 75% of the world shipping tonnage, by deadweight, on international voyages is registered in developing states (Shi and Gullett, 2018, p. 146). This discord however, needs to be resolved in order to follow and adopt the three-step plan of the Initial Strategy, which includes the adoption of possible short-term measures until 2023, possible mid-term measures from 2023 to 2030 and lastly, long-term measures that shall be adopted and effectively start reducing GHG emissions aiming for a zero-carbon or fossil free fuel shipping sector beyond 2030 (IMO Initial Strategy, 2018, Annex 4.1.1). Thereby, short-term measures focus on the enhancement and development of existing measures, whereas possible measures that still need to be developed and agreed upon during the mid-term are highlighted in the timeframe until 2030.

Conclusively, it shall be highlighted that the IMO Initial Strategy is an important step towards the establishment of comprehensive regulatory measures that reflects the goals set out in the Paris Agreement. However, as climate change becomes a more and more important driver for legislative change on the national and international levels, it is likely that these discussions will continue and that pressure will grow on the industry. In fact, the industry is already reacting: in late 2019, the Association of Arctic Expedition Cruise Operators (AECO) anticipated the IMO's ban on heavy fuel oils (HFOs) and decided that its members, cruise ship operators working in the Arctic, would voluntarily refrain from using HFOs (Safety4Sea Editorial Team, 2019). In this way, cruise operators were able to contribute to these ongoing efforts, while local operators of ferries or cargo ships would not yet be forced to take the same action. In semi-structured conversations with industry experts and local residents in Greenland in 2019, it became clear that there are significant concerns that a forced transition to cleaner fuel oils would lead to increasing transport costs and in turn to higher consumer prices in Greenland. These concerns are hardly surprising as most products, including many food products, have to be transported to Greenland by ship and because the trade by ship has long been essentially limited to connections between Denmark and Greenland. Protecting the Arctic marine environment and combating climate change are positive for the local coastal communities in the Arctic because these actions enable the continuation of traditional, sustainable, lifestyles and contribute to food security. But there is also a social dimension to these measures. The transition to a global zero emission society has to take these social aspects into account as well, especially because it is often the case that, like in the Arctic, the communities that suffer the most from the direct and indirect effects of climate change (the indirect effects including the increase in ship traffic in the Arctic Ocean, including 'last minute' Arctic cruise tourism inspired by the impact of climate change that is already visible in the Arctic today) are often not the communities that have created the bulk of the causes for climate change. With regard to the planned ban of HFOs in the Arctic, that follow a similar ban in the Southern Ocean, the delay in the planned implementation might be seen as a recognition of this social dimension because this gives ship operators more time to adapt.

Seafarer Training
But fuel oils, although they are an important aspect of the risk of pollution in the Arctic, are only part of the overall picture. One aspect of navigational safety that has gained more attention after the 2012 *Costa Concordia* disaster is that of the crew. The human factor has already been taken into account for decades in the standardization of training requirements for seafarers in the International Convention on Standards of Training, Certification and Watchkeeping for Seafarers (STCW). Through the Polar Code, additional training requirements for seafarers working in polar regions have been created and while more detailed regulation would have been possible (cf. Kirchner & Pääkkölä, 2016), this has been an important step in the right direction (Kirchner, 2018; Kirchner, 2019).

Enforcing International Legal Standards
All of these norms, however, depend on the flag states' willingness to implement them. It is the legal obligation of the flag state to ensure compliance with international standards by the ships that fly its flag (Scott & VanderZwaag, 2017, p. 727). Today, many ships are registered in countries far from where they operate and the practical ability of flag states to ensure compliance with international environmental standards on faraway high seas is technically limited. In the future, assuming the availability of affordable 24/7 global fast internet connections through satellite constellations, it might be more feasible than today that flag states will impose technological systems (similar to but far more detailed in terms of the types of data transmitted than the automated positioning systems that already are in use today) to increase surveillance of compliance by ships and their crews. But while technical compliance issues can be dealt with through technological solutions, this will not always be the case and it certainly is not the case today. Today, states in different parts of

the world have concluded regional memoranda of understanding (MoUs) that allow for mutual Port State Control (PSC) and effective enforcement of international standards. Ships are subjected to regular controls in foreign ports. Often, these controls are focused on the presence of proper documentation, for example insurance certificates. PSC is an effective way to ensure compliance because vessels can be detained in case of non-compliance, which leads to immediate costs for owners and / or operators, thereby creating a simple financial incentive to comply. Also, due to an exchange of information between different states that are parties to the same MoU, frequent compliance problems will make it more likely for the same vessel to be controlled more often. The shortcoming of this system is that it is often impossible for port authorities in very busy ports to control every ship every time. In particular in the cargo shipping sector, the turnaround times in port are so short that too frequent PSC activities might render a port too unattractive for shipping companies, even in case of perfect compliance, because of the risk of lost profits. Arctic ports that only handle one or few ships at a time might not have this problem and local port authorities, if equipped and funded properly, might be able to devote more time to PSC, thereby increasing the likelihood of identifying, for example, vessels that do not comply with the aforementioned sulphur limits. Already in 2018, the captain of a US cruise vessel was arrested and later fined 100,000 EUR in Marseilles, France, for using fuel with a higher than permitted sulphur-content of 1.68 % instead of the 1.5 % that was permitted in the port at that time (Guardian, 2018). Often, arrests are not even the most potent deterrent, because port authorities may also detain the entire vessel, i.e., making it illegal for the vessel to leave the port. In addition to the loss of profit in the cargo sector, one can easily imagine the financial reputational damage for a cruise ship operating company if hundreds or thousands of passengers will have to be flown out (and compensated) in the middle of an ongoing cruise. The Athens Convention and the 2002 protocol thereto, that also have been implemented into EU law through Regulation (EC) No. 392/2009 of the European Parliament and of the Council of 23 April

2009 on the liability of carriers of passengers by sea in the event of accidents, provide a clear compensation scheme for passengers (see Hoffmann et al., 2013; Kirchner et al., 2015). While the legal obligations depend on flag states insofar as they are the ones that have to ratify international treaties in order to create legal effects for ships that fly their flags, coastal states are by no means powerless.

The Arctic Council
While we all depend on the ocean in one way or another, coastal communities have the greatest interest in the protection of the marine environment. In the Arctic, coastal communities bear the burden of the risks associated with increased maritime traffic (Kirchner, 2016), although the economic benefits are usually enjoyed elsewhere. The coastal states of the Arctic Ocean, i.e., the United States of America, Canada, Denmark with regard to Greenland, Norway, and the Russian Federation, along with Iceland (located in the North Atlantic), as well as Sweden and Finland (coastal states of the Baltic Sea that also often experiences sea ice), have long played a key role in the international governance of the Arctic. Together with six representative organizations of the indigenous peoples of the Arctic (referred to as permanent participants), these states form the Arctic Council (AC), a unique international forum for cooperation on issues of common concern in the Arctic region across political differences. In addition to the aforementioned UNCLOS rules, the member states of the AC have used this forum to negotiate three international treaties: the 2011 Agreement on Cooperation on Aeronautical and Maritime Search and Rescue in the Arctic, the 2013 Agreement on Cooperation on Marine Oil Pollution Preparedness and Response in the Arctic and the 2017 Agreement on Enhancing International Arctic Scientific Cooperation (see Koivurova et al., 2020a, p. 73 et seq.). These treaties all have a strong connection to the sea but also emphasize human-related aspects (see e.g. Rogers et al., 2020), in particular human safety and security. They do not replace UNCLOS but, similar to MARPOL and SOLAS, as well as the Polar Code that is based on both MARPOL and SOLAS, they complement the existing norms.

In these treaties, the strong spirit of cooperation in the Arctic has been given a practical legal form. In addition to that, two of the six working groups of the Arctic Council, the working Group on the Protection of the Arctic Marine Environment (PAME) and the Sustainable Development Working Group (SDWG), have considerably contributed to international developments regarding Arctic marine safety and the protection of the Arctic marine environment. As such, with the publication of the Arctic Marine Shipping Assessment by PAME in 2009, the information included in the report were a valuable contribution of the AC through its Working Group to the negotiations of the Polar Code. This additionally, honoured the recognized need for cooperation of the AC with the IMO regarding shipping activities in the Arctic (AMSA, 2009). Furthermore, several Arctic States have actively contributed to the efforts towards a ban of HFO as a fuel in Arctic shipping. This shows that cooperation between Arctic States extends beyond the auspices of the AC in relation to the protection of the Arctic environment, also in international fora such as the IMO.

Even though the AC is characterized by strong cooperation efforts, it has to be recognized that the AC is not entirely immune against political differences (cf. Arctic Council, 2019), but as long as there is consensus that certain challenges have to be met for the Arctic as a whole, the AC provides a well-functioning forum for international cooperation. While there might be different visions of climate change in the Arctic (cf. Arctic Council, 2019), the protection of the marine environment and of human health as well as the sustainable development of the region (cf. Pongrácz, 2020) are likely to remain shared concerns for the foreseeable future. The same can be said of the need for scientific research in the Arctic Ocean, a field that plays a particularly important role in cross-border cooperation between countries that follow different political trajectories (cf. Berkman, 2020). While the legal status of sustainable development in international law remains the object of some debate (see Boisson de Charzournes & Mbengue, 2020), it has long been a concern for the AC, in addition to the maritime and scientific issues that are already covered by the three aforementioned international treaties that have been concluded by the eight member states of the Arctic Council.

Which Future for Marine Environmental Protection in the Arctic?
What these treaties do not provide is a regional seas agreement (RSA) like it exists for several seas around the world (on the concept see Oral, 2015). Like MARPOL, SOLAS, the Polar Code, and other international legal rules, they form pieces of a puzzle but these pieces together do not yet create a complete picture. Here, it is not only necessary to enforce the existing norms, but there is actually a need for more regulation. International law tends to be slow moving and reactive in nature. This is especially the case when it comes to maritime safety standards. Many technical standards were introduced after specific problems had been identified, for example regarding crew behavior after the *Costa Concordia* disaster, regarding double hulled oil tankers after the 1967 *Torrey Canyon* incident or in connection with roll on/roll off (RoRo) ferries after the fatal sinking of the *Estonia* in 1994. In the Arctic Ocean, the international legal community has reacted to the reality of climate change in the Arctic but can also be seen as having been proactive in terms of regulating some activities that were not yet happening when unregulated fishing was outlawed in the high seas part of the Central Arctic Ocean through the 2018 Agreement to Prevent Unregulated High Seas Fisheries in the Central Arctic Ocean, also referred to as the Central Arctic Ocean Fisheries Agreement (CAOFA). Today, Arctic fisheries regulation (see Hoel, 2020) is actively protecting fish stocks the size and composition of which are still unknown at this time. More often than not, though, international law is reactive. This is also one of the reasons why the Arctic Ocean has not yet been designated a Particularly Sensitive Sea Area (PSSA). Such a measure can be taken once there is a threat from shipping to the marine environment of a sea area. All over the world, sensitive waters have been given this designation to

allow for additional protective measures, so called Associated Protective Measures (APMs). For example, in the Wadden Sea in the North Sea a mandatory route in deeper water that ships are legally required to use and in the Baltic Sea and elsewhere traffic separation schemes have been established so that ships that travel in one direction follow the same route, distinct from the route taken by ships that travel in the opposite direction. These measures can reduce the risk of ship to ship collisions and consequently accident-induced oil spills. Other APMs can consist of reporting schemes to allow coastal states increased marine domain awareness. International law, although defending the general principle of the freedom of navigation, provides coastal states with a wide range of measures to protect the marine environment near to their coasts. Some of these options are included in UNCLOS norms like Article 234 UNCLOS, others contained in other international treaties or in more specific regulations. The protection of the Arctic marine environment remains a work in progress. Although there is no regional seas programme for the Arctic at this time, international law already provides a number of potential approaches to enhance the protection of the fragile environment of the Arctic Ocean.

References

1. Agreement on Cooperation on Aeronautical and Maritime Search and Rescue in the Arctic, adopted 12 May 2011, entered into force 19 January 2013, http://hdl.handle.net/11374/531.
2. Agreement on Cooperation on Marine Oil Pollution Preparedness and Response in the Arctic, adopted 15 May 2013, entered into force 25 March 2016, http://hdl.handle.net/11374/529.
3. Agreement on Enhancing International Arctic Scientific Cooperation, adopted 11 May 2017, entered into force 23 May 2018, https://oaarchive.arctic-council.org/handle/11374/1916.
4. Agreement to Prevent Unregulated High Seas Fisheries in the Central Arctic Ocean [Central Arctic Ocean Fisheries Agreement], adopted 3 October 2018, entered into force 25 June 2021, https://www.mofa.go.jp/files/000449233.pdf.
5. Arctic Council (2019). Joint declarations of the Foreign Ministers of the Arctic States at the 11th Ministerial meeting of the Arctic Council, held in Rovaniemi, Finland, 7 May 2019, http://hdl.handle.net/11374/2418.
6. Arctic Marine Shipping Assessment 2009 Report. Arctic Council, April 2009, second printing, AMSA_2009_Report_2nd_print.pdf.
7. Athens Convention relating to the Carriage of Passengers and their Luggage by Sea (PAL), 1974, 1463 United Nations Treaty Series, No. 24817, https://treaties.un.org/doc/Publication/UNTS/Volume%201463/volume-1463-I-24817-English.pdf.
8. Berkman, Paul Arthur (2020). "Polar science diplomacy", in: Scott, Karen N. & VanderZwaag, David L. (eds.), Research Handbook on Polar Law, Cheltenham: Edward Elgar, pp. 105-123.

9. Boisson de Charzournes, Laurence & Mbengue, Makane Moïse (2020). "Gabčikovo-Nagymaros Project (Hungary/Slovakia) (1997)", in: Bjorge, Eirik & Miles, Cameron (eds.), Landmark Cases in Public International Law, Oxford: Hart, pp. 435-453.
10. Chen, Yuli. (2021). "Reconciling common but differentiated responsibilities principle and no more favourable treatment principle in regulating greenhouse gas emissions from international shipping", in: Marine Policy, 123, 104317.
11. Chircop, Aldo. (2019). "The IMO Initial Strategy for the Reduction of GHGs from International Shipping: A Commentary", in: The International Journal of Marine and Coastal Law, 34(3), 482-512.
12. Convention on the Inter-Governmental Maritime Consultative Organization (London, adopted 6 March 1948, in force 17 March 1958) 289 UNTS 3, as amended and renamed the Convention on the International Maritime Organization, Art. 1(a).
13. [Guardian] The Guardian Staff and Agencies (2018). "Cruise ship captain fined €100,000 for using dirty fuel", in: The Guardian, 26 November 2018, https://www.theguardian.com/world/2018/nov/26/cruise-ship-captain-fined-100000-for-using-dirty-fuel.
14. Hoffmann, Jan Martin Hoffmann, Tüngler, Grit & Kirchner, Stefan (2013). "Europarechtliche Unfallhaftung und Versicherungspflicht der Anbieter von Seereisen", in: 24 Europäische Zeitschrift für Wirtschaftsrecht / European Journal of Business Law / Revue Européenne de Droit Économique (2013), pp. 332-335.
15. Ilulissat Declaration (2008). 28 May 2008, https://arcticportal.org/images/stories/pdf/Ilulissat-declaration.pdf.
16. IMO (MEPC72). 2018. "Resolution MEPC.304(72)." Initial IMO Strategy on Reduction of GHG Emissions from Ships.
17. International Convention for the Prevention of Pollution from Ships (MARPOL), 1973, and Protocol of 1978 Relating

to the International Convention for the Prevention of Pollution from Ships, 1340 United Nations Treaty Series, No. 22484, https://treaties.un.org/doc/Publication/UNTS/Volume%201340/volume-1340-A-22484-English.pdf.
18. International Convention for the Safety of Life at Sea (SOLAS), 1184 United Nations Treaty Series, No. 18961, https://treaties.un.org/doc/Publication/UNTS/Volume%201184/volume-1184-I-18961-English.pdf.
19. International Convention on Standards of Training, Certification and Watchkeeping for Seafarers (STCW), 1978, 1361 United Nations Treaty Series 2, https://treaties.un.org/doc/publication/UNTS/Volume%201361/v1361.pdf.
20. Kahl, Wolfgang & Gärditz, Klaus Ferdinand (2019). Umweltrecht, Munich: C. H. Beck.
21. Kirchner, Stefan (2019). "Disaster Risk Reduction in Cruise Shipping, Capacity Building for Crew Members and the Polar Code", in: Samuel, Katja L. H.; Aronsson-Storrier, Marie & Bookmiller, Kirsten Nakjavani (eds.), The Cambridge Handbook of Disaster Risk Reduction and International Law, Cambridge: Cambridge University Press, pp. 336-351, https://doi.org/10.1017/9781108564540.019.
22. Kirchner, Stefan (2016). "Multiple Risks and Limited Law: Compensation for Oil Spills in the Context of Long-Term Damages to Arctic Coastal Communities", in: 30 Ocean Yearbook, pp. 267-281.
23. Kirchner, Stefan (2018). "The human dimension of the Polar Code", in: 10 Australian Journal of Maritime & Ocean Affairs, pp. 1-8, https://doi.org/10.1080/18366503.2017.1333191.
24. Kirchner, Stefan & Pääkkölä, Susanna (2019). "A New Ocean: Human Safety in Arctic Cruise Tourism", in: 31 University of San Francisco Maritime Law Journal, pp. 1-17.

25. Kirchner, Stefan & Pääkkölä, Susanna (2016). "Polar Health Risks: Seafarers' Rights and Training in International Law", in: 28 University of San Francisco Maritime Law Journal, pp. 225-235.
26. Kirchner, Stefan; Tüngler, Grit & Hoffmann, Jan Martin (2015). "Carrier Liability for Damages incurred by Ship Passengers: The European Union as a Trailblazer towards a Global Liability Regime?", in: 23 University of Miami International and Comparative Law Review, pp. 193-214.
27. Koivurova, Timo; Kirchner, Stefan & Kleemola-Juntunen, Pirjo (2020). "Are we ready to govern a new ocean?", in: Chantal Ribeiro, Marta; Loureiro Bastos, Fernando; Henriksen, Tore (eds.). Global Challenges and the Law of the Sea. Cham: Springer, pp. 59-80.
28. Koivurova, Timo; Kleemola-Juntunen, Pirjo & Kirchner, Stefan (2020a). "Arctic regional agreements and arrangements", in: Scott, Karen N. & VanderZwaag, David L. (eds.), Research Handbook on Polar Law, Cheltenham: Edward Elgar, pp. 64-83.
29. Koivurova, Timo; Kleemola-Juntunen, Pirjo & Kirchner, Stefan (2019). "Emergence of a New Ocean: How to React to the Massive Change?", in: Coats, K. S. & Holroyd, C. (eds.), The Palgrave Handbook of Arctic Policy and Politics, Basingstoke: Palgrave Macmillan, pp. 409-425.
30. MEPC 67/INF.3 Third IMO GHG Study 2014 – Final Report, International Maritime Organization (IMO), London, 2014.
31. Oral, Nilufer (2015). "Forty years of the UNEP Regional Seas Programme: from past to future", in: Rayfuse, Rosemary (ed.), Research Handbook on International Marine Environmental Law, Cheltenham: Edward Elgar, pp. 339-362.
32. PAME (2020). "Arctic Shipping Status Report #1", THE INCREASE IN ARCTIC SHIPPING 2013-2019 (arcticcouncil.org).

33. Paris Agreement, 12 December 2015, UN Doc FCCC/CP/2015/10/Add.1.
34. Polar Code, MEPC 68/21/Add. 1, Annex 10, pp. 3-55, http://www.imo.org/en/MediaCentre/HotTopics/polar/Documents/POLAR%20CODE%20TEXT%20AS%20ADOPTED.pdf.
35. Pongrácz, Eva (2020). "Sustainability in an Arctic Context: Resilience of the Arctic Marine Environment", in: Pongrácz, Eva; Pavlov, Victor & Hänninen, Niko (eds.), Arctic Marine Sustainability - Arctic Maritime Businesses and the Resilience of the Marine Environment, Cham: Springer Nature, pp. 3-23.
36. Protocol of 2002 to the Athens Convention relating to the Carriage of Passengers and their Luggage by Sea, 1974, http://www.transportrecht.org/dokumente/AthenProt2002e.pdf.
37. Regulation (EC) No. 392/2009 of the European Parliament and of the Council of 23 April 2009 on the liability of carriers of passengers by sea in the event of accidents, Official Journal 2009 L 131/24, https://eur-lex.europa.eu/LexUriServ/LexUriServ.do?uri=OJ:L:2009:131:0024:0046:EN:PDF.
38. Ringbom, Henrik (2015). "Vessel-source pollution", in: Rayfuse, Rosemary (ed.), Research Handbook on International Marine Environmental Law, Cheltenham: Edward Elgar, pp. 105-131.
39. Rogers, Derek D.; King, Michael & Carnahan, Heather (2020). "Arctic Search and Rescue: A Case Study for Understanding Issues Related to Training and Human Factors When Working in the North", in: Pongrácz, Eva; Pavlov, Victor & Hänninen, Niko (eds.), *Arctic Marine Sustainability - Arctic Maritime Businesses and the Resilience of the Marine Environment*, Cham: Springer Nature, pp. 333-344.

40. Safety4Sea Editorial Team (2019). "AECO to apply self-imposed ban on HFO in the Arctic", in: Safety4Sea, 12 November 2019, https://safety4sea.com/aeco-to-apply-self-imposed-ban-on-hfo-in-the-arctic/?__cf_chl_jschl_tk__=pmd_l2c56UbfIYeCU99NSbKy0pH9GhToqB6NWzIkENhnsbU-1635314683-0-gqNtZGzNAlCjcnBszQi9 (last visited 27 October 2021).
41. Scott, Karen N. & VanderZwaag, David L. (2017). "Polar Oceans and the Law of the Sea", in: Rothwell, Donald R., Oude Elferink, Alex G., Scott, Karen N. & Stephens, Tim (eds)., The Oxford Handbook of the Law of the Sea, Oxford: Oxford University Press, pp. 724-751.
42. Shi, Yubing, & Gullett, Warwick. (2018). "International regulation on low-carbon shipping for climate change mitigation: development, challenges, and prospects.", Ocean Development & International Law, 49(2), 134-156.
43. United Nations Convention on the Law of the Sea, adopted 10 December 1982, entered into force 16 November 1994, 1833 United Nations Treaty Series 3, https://treaties.un.org/doc/Publication/UNTS/Volume%201833/volume-1833-A-31363-English.pdf.
44. Wadhams, Peter (2017). A Farewell to Ice – A Report from the Arctic. London: Penguin Books.

LEGALITY OF FOREIGN MILITARY ACTIVITIES IN THE EXCLUSIVE ECONOMIC ZONE: LESSONS LEARNED FROM THE 2020 BERING SEA INCIDENT

Medy Dervovic & Pavel Tkach

Abstract: In a changing era deeply impacted by climate change, navigational, economic, and military activities are rapidly emerging in the Arctic. To avoid recreating conflicts involving competing uses of the Exclusive Economic Zones (EEZs), this chapter endeavors to analyze factually and legally Russian military maneuvers performed in the Bering Sea under the Ocean Shield 2020 exercises. In particular, the focus is placed on the incident between US-flagged fishing vessels and Russian military vessels and aircraft in the border area of the Russian and the US EEZs. While the legality of foreign military activities in the EEZ is subject to certain conditions in the international law of the sea, this chapter concludes that circumstantial elements related to prior notification through appropriate communication channels and the establishment of maritime exclusion/safety zones influence the aforementioned legality in practice. Eventually, lessons drawn from the analysis of this incident shall guide the shaping of safety and security dimensions of Arctic governance.
Keywords: Military activities, Exclusive Economic Zone (EEZ), Law of the sea, Bering Sea, Arctic governance

Introduction

Prior to the creation of the exclusive economic zones (EEZs), the concept *mare liberum* largely prevailed in waters beyond the territorial seas through the freedoms of the high seas and knew, therefore, little to no restrictions. Nevertheless, the introduction of EEZs in 1982 established a *sui generis* legal regime applicable to the waters situated up to 200 nautical miles from the baselines. Therein, coastal States enjoy sovereign rights over living and non-living resources characterized by their economic potential. They also exercise jurisdiction over specific activities and on the protection and preservation of the marine environment. Noticeably, the EEZ legal regime leaves unclear the treatment of foreign military activities. On this complex question, a divide exists within the legal doctrine supported by valid and thought-provoking arguments. While some admit the legality of peaceful military maneuvers and exercises in the EEZ of another State (Quéneudec, 1982), others refuse it completely (Karagiannis, 2004), and other scholars only reiterate the intricacy inherent to the performance of such activities in a zone of sovereign rights and jurisdiction regulated by a silent legal framework in this regard (Cave de De la Maza, 1998).

In this context, this chapter will look at the military activities performed by the Russian Federation in the Bering Sea under the Ocean Shield 2020 exercises. In particular, this chapter will focus on the incident that occurred within the US EEZ and compromised both the safety and freedoms of navigation and fishing of US-flagged fishing vessels.

In light of the 2020 incident, the authors will explore to what extent the Russian military exercises in the Bering Sea were or could be considered lawful according to the international law of the sea. The findings of this chapter shall guide the development of Arctic navigation and contribute to the shaping of an advanced governance regime for safety and security in the Arctic. After presenting a contextual overview and the characteristics of Ocean Shield 2020 and the incident under review, the authors will assess the legality of these activities as foreign military activities in the EEZ and consider the impact of surrounding elements on the said legality, before offering conclusions.

Overview of the 2020 Incident in the US EEZ

It is crucial to characterize the Russian military activities in the US EEZ during the Ocean Shield 2020 naval exercises for the legal analysis of the said activities. Then, the geographical contextualization of the incident and the description of the main contention points between the Russian Federation and the United States of America are essential elements to understand the issue at stake.

Characterizing Russian Military Exercises under Ocean Shield 2020

The Russian military activities under the Ocean Shield 2020 framework will be described as constituting military training and analyzed as peaceful military maneuvers and exercises at sea.

In August 2020, the Russian Navy conducted the Ocean Shield 2020 training exercises in the Russian and the US EEZs. The Commander-in-Chief of the Navy of the Russian Federation, Admiral Nikolai Yevmenov, said that more than 50 warships and about 40 aircraft were taking part in the exercises in the Bering Sea, which involved multiple practice missile launches (The Associated Press, 2020).

This naval training had five major tasks to practice: (1) "[t]he integrated training of amphibious landings protected by naval artillery gunfire from small warships" (Sukhankin, 2020), (2) "[t]he integrated use of surface and sub-surface naval forces". During this part of the exercise, "the missile cruiser "Varyag" and the nuclear-powered cruise missile submarine "Omsk" jointly fired at targets located in open water in the Bering Sea" (Sukhankin, 2020), (3) the use of Unmanned Aerial Vehicles (UAVs) such as an Orlan-10, a medium-range, multi-purpose UAV which was "employed to correct naval gunfire aiming at hidden, coastal targets that could not be spotted by the naval forces due to the challenging local geographic conditions" (Sukhankin, 2020), (4) "[t]he improvement of naval logistics and transportation capabilities. In this regard, the key role was ascribed to [a] large landing ship [to rehearse] loading military equipment and personnel from the unequipped coast" (Sukhankin, 2020), and (5) naval aviation practices of MiG-31 and Il-38 aircraft (Sukhankin, 2020).

The peaceful use of the seas is a fundamental principle found throughout the 1982 United Nations Convention on the Law of the Sea (on peaceful uses, see UNCLOS, 1982: Preamble, Article 301, Annex VI; on peaceful purposes, see UNCLOS, 1982: Articles 88, 141, 143, 147(2)(d), 155(2), 240(a), 242(1) and 246(3)). While it is certain that the notion of peaceful uses of the seas do not exclude all military activities (Tsarev, 1988, p. 156), it is not always easy to define whether a specific military activity is peaceful or not. Nonetheless, regarding military maneuvers and exercises, their compatibility with UNCLOS in general appears to be confirmed in academic literature (Geng, 2012, p. 27). It follows that to be prohibited, a military activity would need to represent an act of aggression (Francioni, 1985, p. 223).

When considering that the military maneuvers and exercises of Ocean Shield 2020 were part of a training aiming at assessing and improving arms control in the navigational conditions of the Arctic, no aggression characteristic shows through *per se*. Moreover, the launching components were not directed towards any vessel or State. Therefore, the Russian military activities under Ocean Shield 2020 could be interpreted, at least in theory, as belonging to the category of peaceful military activities.

Contextual and Factual Analysis of the Incident
The location of the incident bears particular significance on the perceived legality of the Russian military activities and helps highlight contention points. The Baker-Shevardnadze line (Map 1, 1990, IX) delimits the US/USSR EEZs in the Bering Sea as provided in the Agreement between the United States of America and the Union of Soviet Socialist Republics on the maritime boundary (US/USSR Agreement, 1990). Building on diverging interpretations of the 1867 maritime boundary (US-Russia Convention, 1867; Konyshev & Sergunin, 2014, p. 60), the 1990 Baker-Shevardnadze line is the result of compromises (Konyshev & Sergunin, 2014, p. 60 et seq.). It did not prevent Konstantin Kosachev, the Chair of the Foreign Affairs Committee of the Federation Council, from qualifying the Agreement as a betrayal of the Soviet Union (Artamonov, 2020). Indeed, a particularity of the US/USSR Agreement resides in delimiting the Eastern and Western Special Areas according to Articles 3 (1) and (2). These areas correspond to mutual cessions of EEZ sovereign rights and jurisdiction over portions of EEZ extending beyond the Baker-Shevardnadze line to the other riparian State. Article 3 (3)

of the Agreement specifies that these cessions cannot represent an extension of the EEZ beyond 200 nautical miles *per se*. Nevertheless, the State Duma of the Russian Federation argues that through this Agreement, it lost 31.4 thousand square kilometers of EEZ (State Duma, 2002; Konyshev & Sergunin, 2014, p. 63) of great strategic and economic importance (Artamonov, 2020). It also contends that the US EEZ exceed 200 nautical miles because of "unjustifiably ceded area of soviet exclusive economic zone" (State Duma, 2002: 2). For its part, the United States of America appears to have a better understanding of the implications of this Agreement because the National Ocean and Atmospheric Administration affirms the US EEZ "extends no more than 200 nautical miles from the territorial sea baseline" (NOAA, n.d.).

However, the incident did not occur within any of these special areas but in the US EEZ, close to the Baker-Shevardnadze line (see North Pacific Fishery Management Council, 2020, Map).

On 26 August 2020, Russian warships and aircraft encountered US-flagged fishing vessels legally fishing in the US EEZ (North Pacific Fishery Management Council, 2020). During that day, the Russian naval warships and aircraft directed these US fishing vessels to depart from the area due to safety concerns associated with a missile launch (North Pacific Fishery Management Council, 2020). According to a testimony to the Subcommittee on Security of the US Senate Committee on Commerce, Science, and Transportation on 22 September 2020, the Russian warships requested the fishing vessels to leave for safety reasons (Madsen, 2020). Fearing for their safety, the US captains and their crew left the area as requested by the Russian vessels. *Madsen* also mentions that the decision to leave "cost companies hundreds of thousands of dollars in lost fishing opportunities" (Madsen, 2020, p. 3) and gear (Hagenbuch, 2020). The perspective of both sides regarding the incident are as follows:

The Alaska command at the joint Elmendorf-Richardson base in Anchorage knew about "naval exercises". Russian side sent a prior notification about exercises, and the purpose of initiated radio contact was a notification about the danger of exercises. After notification

from fishing vessels on Russian vessels' presence, the Coast Guard contacted the Elmendorf-Richardson base, which stated that the Russian naval ships were in the region to participate in the exercise (Rybolovstvo i Rybovodstvo, 2020).
The US fishing vessels operated lawfully within the US EEZ and could not be ordered to "leave". United States Coast Guard personnel did not appear to know that a major Russian military exercise was underway in the US EEZ. Russia provided notice of its intent to conduct these exercises, including specific coordinates, *via* Hydrographic Warning-Pacific Ocean (HYDROPAC). The fishing industry does not regularly monitor the HYDROPAC system, and it does not constitute sufficient notice to mariners. Furthermore, it is worth mentioning that HYDROPAC notice was received by at least one agency of the US government (Rybolovstvo i Rybovodstvo, 2020). Both perspectives pay attention to the advance notice in military exercises. Through the analysis of both positions, three issues can be identified in the actions related to the notification about upcoming naval exercise: (1) the Russian Federation first notified the US naval base responsible for naval control of the US waters surrounding Alaska, but not responsible for the notification of commercial vessels on safety measures related to military exercises in neighboring maritime areas; (2) the Russian notification of military exercises to the US Coast Guard through HYDROPAC turns out to be inappropriate. Indeed, in 2018, the US Department of Homeland Security issued a notice of termination of U.S. Coast Guard rebroadcast of Hydrographic Warning-Atlantic Ocean (HYDROLANT) and HYDROPAC information (US Coast Guard, 2018). This notice transferred the obligation of rebroadcasting to the National Geospatial-Intelligence Agency (US Coast Guard, 2018); (3) After receiving the notification from the Russian side, the joint Elmendorf-Richardson base contacted the US Coast Guard to add Russian naval exercise to the navigational schedule. However, the US Coast Guard did not go through with the update. Four months after the incident, this was confirmed by the then Vice Commandant of the US Coast Guard, Admiral Charles Ray. Ray was aware that Russian military

activities were ongoing in the area, but the Bering Sea fishing industry was not informed (Ruskin, 2020). The Vice Commandant even stated, "This was not our best day, with regards to doing our role to look after American fishermen […]" and admitted responsibly as follows: "I will just be quite frank: We own some of this" (Ruskin, 2020).

Insufficient and negligent advanced notice on naval exercises led to the necessity to limit the freedoms of navigation and fisheries of US fishing vessels in the US EEZ. Following the factual analysis and characterization of Russia's Ocean Shield 2020 exercises in the Bering Sea, a legal assessment is thus required to evaluate the legality of such military activities in US EEZ.

Assessing the Legality of Russian Military Exercises and Maneuvers in the US EEZ

The incident under study raises the question of the legality of foreign military activities in the EEZ under the United Nations Convention on the Law of the Sea (UNCLOS, 1982). More specifically, this section addresses the deliberate ambiguity embedded in the legal regime of EEZs in this regard. Then, to objectively assess the legality of Russian military exercises in the US EEZ, the authors will focus on the impact of selected circumstantial elements affecting the legality of foreign military activities in the EEZ.

The Deliberately Ambiguous Legal Regime of Foreign Military Activities in the EEZ

In 1982, the introduction of the notion of EEZ deeply transformed the law of the sea. While the scope of the legal regime of EEZ revolves around the sovereign rights of coastal States over economic uses of the EEZ *lato sensu*, it nonetheless safeguards rights and acknowledges residual rights for other States.

General Framework
When analyzing the scope of coastal States' rights and jurisdiction in the EEZ, one has to distinguish this maritime zone from other maritime zones under coastal States' sovereignty and jurisdiction because of its multifunctional nature (Kwiatkowska, 1989, p. 4). The EEZ is engineered as a spatial extension of coastal States' sovereign rights over living and non-living resources (UNCLOS, Article 56(1)(a)) located in waters reaching up to 200 nautical miles from the baseline (UNCLOS, Article 57). As a result, the EEZ regime displays a strong emphasis on the economic potential of these resources. In particular, coastal States derive their sovereign rights over natural resources in the EEZ from their economic potential rather than territorial sovereignty or geographic proximity alone (Proelss, 2017, p. 425).

Article 56(1)(a) UNCLOS outlines the sovereign rights of coastal States in their EEZ in a non-exhaustive manner. In a nutshell, these exclusively include exploratory, exploiting, conservatory, and managing rights of natural resources located in the water column, seabed, and subsoil or the EEZ.

Albeit providing for a wide range of sovereign rights for coastal States, the EEZ is not a zone of sovereignty as rightly recalled by the 1985 arbitral award on the delimitation of the maritime boundary between Guinea and Guinea-Bissau (Guinea/Guinea-Bissau, 1985, para. 124). Consequently, coastal States do not have absolute control over all uses of the sea in the EEZ. This is further acknowledged by the list of competences attributed to coastal States in Article 56 UNCLOS, which is characterized by its limiting nature (Beckman & Davenport, 2012, pp. 7-10). Furthermore, stemming from the reading of Article 59 UNCLOS, it is apparent that some rights or jurisdiction could, in theory, be unattributed by UNCLOS. The EEZ legal regime thus highlights the existence of residual rights for other States. Perhaps the most symptomatic example of activities not precisely forecasted by UNCLOS is military activities performed in the EEZ of another coastal State. It is the case because military uses of the seas were only marginally addressed during the Third United Nations Conference on the Law of Sea (Dupuy & Vignes, 1991, pp. 1234, 1247).

The question of foreign military activities in the EEZ fueled numerous academic debates on the legality of such activities and the extent of sovereign rights and jurisdiction of coastal States in this regard. A clear and long-lasting divergence exists, both in state practice and in academic writings (discussed later).

A minority of States is of the view that foreign military activities in their EEZ are subject to prior consent or authorization (Rigaldies, 1997, p. 21 (there fn. 40); Geng, 2012, pp. 25-26) whereas the majority of States advocate against such infringement to the freedom of navigation (Geng, 2012, pp. 25-26; Pedrozo, 2014, pp. 515-516). The United States of America follows the second view (Rigaldies, 1997, pp. 39; United Nations Secretariat, 1983, p. 244).

Here, the point of contention mainly relates to the declarations made by the minority of States when signing and ratifying UNCLOS. As recalled by Geng (Geng, 2012, p. 25), UNCLOS was conceived as a package deal to which States could not subtract themselves from certain obligations (Article 309 UNCLOS). However, Article 310 UNCLOS safeguards the right of States parties to make declarations and statements. The only condition laid out by UNCLOS highlights the necessity for these declarations and statements to not impair or empty the Convention of its substance (Article 310 UNCLOS). Concerning the declarations requiring seeking consent before operating military activities in a foreign EEZ, Rigaldies (Rigaldies, 1997, p. 39, there fn. 106) argues that while such declarations do not infringe UNCLOS *per se*, their implementation represents a risk in practice.

Residual Right to Perform Foreign Military Activities in the EEZ
The residual nature of the right to perform military activities in foreign EEZ originates in the silence of UNCLOS in this regard due to the difficult and brief apprehension of this subject during the negotiations. Nonetheless, through an interpretative effort of the phrases "other internationally lawful uses of the sea" and "due regard" in

Article 58 UNCLOS, it becomes possible to explore and draw the outline of the legality of foreign military activities in the EEZ.

Article 58 UNCLOS addresses the rights and duties of other States in the EEZ. Its first paragraph establishes a non-exhaustive list of competences that remarkably ends by providing that all States can enjoy "other internationally lawful uses of the sea related to [the] freedoms [of the high seas referred to in Article 87 UNCLOS], such as those associated with the operations of ships, aircraft [...], and compatible with other provisions of this Convention". To determine whether peaceful military activities —such as those performed by the Russian Federation under the Ocean Shield 2020 framework— fit in this broad category, one must identify the characteristics of peaceful military activities. It is important to note that there is a general consensus that military and economic activities can coexist in the EEZ (Rose, 1990, p. 129; Francioni, 1985, p. 214). In this context, and considering the doctrinal debate exposed hereinafter, the notion of "other internationally lawful uses of the sea" (Article 58 UNCLOS) appears, nonetheless, too complex to be interpreted uniformly.

On the one hand, one can argue that because navigation is not included within Article 56 UNCLOS on the rights, jurisdiction, and duties of coastal States in the EEZ, coastal States do not have the legitimate authority to regulate navigation therein (Quéneudec, 1982, p. 323). According to Quéneudec (Quéneudec 1982, p. 322), military activities *lato sensu* are part of the freedom of navigation and overflight, and he also acknowledges their inherently lawful character. Moreover, he affirms that the right to perform military activities at sea beyond territorial waters is based on customary international law (Quéneudec, 1982, p. 322) as recalled by the International Court of Justice in the Corfu Channel case opposing the United Kingdom and Albania (ICJ, 1949, p. 22).

On the other hand, another scholar deconstructs the notion of military activities because it would be wrong to govern all military activities the same way due to the diverse and broad spectrum of activities this notion encompasses (Karagiannis, 2004, p. 361), beyond mere military defense. While assimilating the simple and continuous passage of military vessels in the EEZ as another internationally lawful use of the sea in conformity with Article 87 UNCLOS (Karagiannis, 2004, p. 365; Proelss, 2017, p. 453), Karagiannis does not recognize military maneuvers as a part of the freedom of navigation. His reasoning lies in the fact that the conduct of military activities usually implies the establishment, *de facto* or *de jure*, of restrictions on navigation for safety purposes, thus impeding the freedom of navigation of other vessels (Karagiannis, 2004, p. 368; the legality of this category of military activities characterized by the temporary infringement on normal uses of the EEZ by other States has always been difficult to recognize, see Dupuy & Vignes, 1991, p. 1253). Furthermore, the association of these military maneuvers to the operation of ships and aircraft in the sense of Article 58 (1) UNCLOS appears intricate. Indeed, where the English term 'operation' can accommodate military maneuvers to some extent, the term used in the French version of UNCLOS introduces a commercial connotation ('exploitation') instead (Karagiannis, 2004, p. 368). Here, it should be noted that both the English and French versions of UNCLOS are authentic texts with none prevailing over the other (Article 320 UNCLOS). They are, therefore, of equal authoritative value according to Article 33 (1) of the Vienna Convention on the Law of Treaties (Vienna Convention, 1969). However, Article 33 (3) presumes the consistency of the meaning of the terms used in the different authentic versions of a treaty. The slight discrepancy observed above might not be as significant as initially foreseen but could be helpful when interpreting the meaning of Article 58 (1) UNCLOS.

In between these opposite positions prevails the impossibility to consider all military activities in the EEZ as included in Article 58 (1) with certainty (Proelss, 2017, p. 453; Beckman and Davenport, 2012, pp. 24-27). Nevertheless, States have the right to perform, if not all, a wide array of military activities in the EEZ of another State as long as (i) they do not consist in the threat of or the use of force, (ii) take into account the rights of the coastal State and other States, and (iii) are in conformity with international law (Cave de De la Maza, 1998,

p. 148). Subsequently, the concept of due regard needs to be further analyzed as a supplementary element framing the residual right of foreign military activities in the EEZ.

Within the context of EEZs, the "due regard" clauses in Articles 56 (2) and 58 (3) UNCLOS elaborate a balance between the rights and obligations of coastal States and other States based on reciprocity and mutual obligations (Oxman, 2018, p. 115). Through this legal mechanism accommodating inherently different interests, these due regard clauses introduce the principle of reasonableness of competing uses in the EEZs (Kwiatkowska, 1989, p. 214). Interestingly, the insertion of these clauses, coupled with the intentionally limited wording of Article 58 (1) UNCLOS, strongly reaffirm that coastal States' rights and jurisdiction in the EEZ are not absolute (Proelss, 2017, p. 430). It thus favors a permissive interpretation of the EEZ legal regime recognizing the legality of foreign military activities in the EEZ under some conditions.

Acknowledging the wording and configuration of both articles, it is clear that due regard has to be given to the rights and duties attributed under the EEZ legal regime. Therefore, for third States, due regard must be paid to the rights and obligations relevant to coastal States' sovereign rights and jurisdiction over EEZ natural resources and other activities mentioned in Article 56 UNCLOS (Beckman & Davenport, 2012, p. 11). Put differently, this due regard clause implies that States shall avoid and refrain from interfering with the rights and duties of coastal States over EEZ resources while using foreign EEZ according to the framework set up in Article 58 UNCLOS (Cave de De la Maza, 1998, p. 143).

In theory, the standard aimed by the due regard clause in Article 58 UNCLOS does not cover the security interests of coastal States in their EEZ (Beckman & Davenport, 2012, p. 11). Nevertheless, in practice, circumstances should dictate the intensity of regard expected from a foreign State when using the EEZ (Kunoy, 2017, p. 397). For instance, when a State conducts military activities in a foreign EEZ that carries a high level of risk, such as weapon testing, the said State should take measures ensuring the safety of maritime navigation (Geng, 2012, p. 27). In this case, due regard would be paid not only to other users of the EEZ in question, but also to non-economic interests of the coastal State related, *inter alia*, to the protection and preservation of the marine environment (Article 56 (1) (b) (iii) UNCLOS). In this scenario, measures to consider would range from sufficient warning through appropriate communication channels to the creation of temporary safety zones. In parallel, these essential measures must, at all times, respect coastal States' sovereign rights and duties. In determining the imperative nature of such measures, the scope and nature of the military activity, its proximity to vessels of the coastal States, and its potential impact on the marine environment (Geng 2012, p. 27) are useful parameters to assess the circumstances and the legality of certain military activities.

In light of this legal framework and the factual description of the incident, the following section attempts to objectively assess the circumstantial elements impacting the legality of Russian military activities. Eventually, it will provide insights on alternatives that could strengthen the legality of these operations.

Circumstantial Elements Impacting the Legality of Foreign Military Activities in the EEZ

Given the nature of Russian military activities in the US EEZ and the issue they raised in practice, the authors chose to concentrate on communication channels and maritime exclusion or safety zones as circumstantial elements potentially affecting the legality of foreign military activities in the EEZ.

Appropriate Communication Channels

In 1979, the Inter-Governmental Maritime Consultative Organization (IMCO), known today as the International Maritime Organization (IMO), established the World-Wide Navigational Warning Service (WWNWS) in a joint effort with the International Hydrographic Organization (IHO) (IMCO, 1979). The purpose of WWNWS is to coordinate navigational warnings in the most efficient manner possible, for safety reasons, and through notably the standardization of methods used to broadcast warnings, including the formats and content of messages (Soluri, 1998, pp. 15-16). The facilitation of the coordination process through the zoning of the seas identified 16 geographical areas called NAVAREA (IMCO, 1979, Article 2.1.3. and related Appendix).

To reinforce the coordination of navigational warnings, the International Convention for the Safety of Life at Sea (SOLAS) provides the obligation for every ship to be equipped with a broadcast system in order to be informed of safety warnings in the area in which the vessel is navigating (SOLAS, 1974, Chapter IV, Regulation 12.2). Since 1999, appropriate broadcasting systems for navigational warnings include NAVTEX and SafetyNET (IMO, 1991, para. 3.1).

When observing a map representing the radio navigational warning systems, it is noticeable that where HYDROPAC is the warning system to use in the Russian part of the Bering Sea -NAVAREA XIII-, the US part of the Bering Sea -NAVAREA XII- uses its own warning system (NGA, no date). Arguably, warning the future conduct of military activities in the EEZ of another coastal State through an inappropriate communication channel could tarnish the legality of these activities, especially when they pose a threat to the sovereign rights of the coastal State in its EEZ and to vessels navigating therein. That said, the coordination and the implementation of the communication system should be effective. As indicated earlier in this chapter, it does not appear to have been the case during the 2020 incident.

Even beyond the issues of the legality of Russian military activities in the US EEZ and the hierarchization of competing uses in the EEZ (*i.e.*, whether economic uses prevail over non-economic uses in the EEZ), the 2020 incident challenges the efficiency of the WWNWS and calls for a reinforced standardization of navigational warning systems for safety and security reasons at sea.

Maritime Exclusion or Safety Zones

In an attempt to accommodate the freedoms of navigation and fishing with the right to perform foreign military activities in the EEZ, a closer look at the notion of maritime exclusion or safety zones appears relevant.

Unfortunately, UNCLOS does not contain any explicit provision on the right for States performing military activities in another State's EEZ to establish maritime exclusion or safety zones therein. In the EEZ, coastal States are the only ones allowed to create these zones, notably around the artificial islands, installations, and structures mentioned in Article 56 (1) UNCLOS. Thus, in the present incident, even if the Russian Federation were to have established a safety zone around its military vessels, its enforcement would have to rest on common sense rather than proper legal foundations (see Karagiannis, 2004, p. 367).

There is no evidence of the creation of a maritime exclusion zone around the area where Russian vessels were performing military activities. Nonetheless, the prior warning through an appropriate communication channel can *de facto* translate into a temporary maritime exclusion zone. This argument follows the common-sense logic adopted by Karagiannis (Karagiannis, 2004, p. 367). Assuming that the military activities in the US EEZ were properly communicated in advance, vessels around the forecasted exercise area would simply avoid it for the sake of primary safety considerations.

However, in a maritime zone fundamentally dominated by sovereign rights over resources, the legality of military activities severely impairing fishing rights is doubtful. This is especially flagrant considering the ambiguous and residual status of foreign military activities in EEZs compared to the explicit and quintessential nature of resource rights in Part V of UNCLOS.

Conclusion

If one were to adopt a restrictive approach to considering military activities as a manifestation of the freedom of navigation, there would be no doubt regarding the unlawful character of foreign military activities in the EEZ. However, when considering foreign military activities in the EEZ as a lawful component of the freedom of navigation, the question of the legality of Russian naval exercises in the US EEZ is to be answered quite differently. States performing peaceful foreign military activities in the EEZ must pay due regard to the rights and duties of the coastal State attributed by UNCLOS. Depending on the circumstances, additional measures to protect the economic and environmental interests of the riparian State and ensure the safety of other users of the EEZ may need to be undertaken. Building on the experience of the 2020 incident in the Bering Sea, additional measures encompass *inter alia* prior notification of upcoming military exercises and/or the establishment of maritime exclusion or safety zones. To be deemed appropriate, however, prior notification must be carried out via appropriate communication channels. Otherwise, incidents like the one reviewed here would keep occurring. Moreover, and regardless of their legal foundation, the effectiveness of maritime exclusion/safety zones heavily rests on warning notifications being properly communicated and transmitted to the relevant authority in charge of updating navigation schedules. By acknowledging these elements, it appears that both States involved in the incident acted negligently.

To reduce the likelihood of similar conflicts of uses in the EEZ questioning the very legality of military activities from happening, a better standardization or harmonization of notification and communication systems in the Bering Sea would be beneficial. Another opportunity would reside in bilateral or international efforts to establish detailed instructions regarding prior notification and maritime exclusion/safety zones when conducting foreign military activities in EEZs. In practice, inspiration can be found in the bilateral effort between India and Pakistan to adopt an agreement on advanced notice (India-Pakistan Agreement, 1991).

Prior notification proved to be an essential safeguard for the freedom of navigation of warships. On 25 November 2018, the Russian Federation limited the freedom of navigation of Ukrainian military vessels which planned to transit from the port of Odesa to the port of Mariupol in the Azov Sea (Aksenov, 2018) despite the existence of a bilateral agreement between the Russian Federation and Ukraine granting warships of both nations the right to navigate freely the Azov Sea (Russia/Ukraine Agreement, 2003, Article 2 (1)). Following the Russian position, this limitation originated from the lack of appropriate prior notification of navigation of Ukrainian vessels to the Russian port authorities which construed it as a threat.

These incidents and proposed remedies shall help alleviate future difficulties regarding the interpretation of the equivocal notion of "other internationally lawful uses of the sea". The 2020 incident also emphasizes the reciprocal nature of the due regard principle embedded in the EEZ legal regime.

Eventually, such lessons shall guide future security and safety practices in the Arctic given the increase of military exercises therein, and navigational and economic prospects offered by the melting Arctic Ocean.

References

1. Aksenov, P. (2018, November 26). Инцидент в Керченском проливе: кто прав? [The Kerch Strait Incident : Who Is Right ?]. *BBC News*. https://www.bbc.com/russian/features-46343093 [in Russian].
2. Artamonov (2020, February 10). «Линия предательства»: Шеварднадзе украл у России часть Берингова моря ["Line of Betrayal": Shevardnadze Stole Part of the Bering Sea from Russia]. *Zvezda*. https://zvezdaweekly.ru/news/20201311536-Zuqnn.html [in Russian].
3. Beckman, R. & Davenport, T. (2012). The EEZ Regime: Reflections After 30 Years. In *Proceedings from the 2012 LOSI-KIOST Conference on Securing the Ocean for the Next Generation*. Available at: https://www.law.berkeley.edu/files/Beckman-Davenport-final.pdf.
4. Cave de De la Maza, R. (1998). Los Usos Militares de la Zona Economica Exclusiva [Military Uses in the Exclusive Economic Zone]. *Revista de Marina*, 843(2), 136-150. [in Spanish].
5. Dupuy, R.-J. & Vignes, D. (1991). Peaceful Uses of the Sea, Denuclearization and Disarmament. In Dupuy, R.-J. & Vignes, D. (Eds.), *A Handbook on the New Law of the Sea* (Volume 2, pp. 1233-1320). Martinus Nijhoff Publishers.
6. Federal law (1995). Federal Law of 15.07.1995 N 101-FZ, as amended on 08.12.2020, on International Treaties of the Russian Federation.
7. Francioni, F. (1985). Peacetime Use of Force, Military Activities, and the New Law of the Sea. *Cornell International Law Journal*, 18(2), 203-226.
8. Geng, J. (2012). The Legality of Foreign Military Activities in the Exclusive Economic Zone Under UNCLOS. *Merkourios*, 28(74), 22-30.

9. Guinea/Guinea-Bissau (1985). Case Concerning the Delimitation of the Maritime Boundary Between Guinea and Guinea-Bissau, 14 February 1985. In United Nations, *Reports of International Arbitral Awards/Recueil des Sentences Arbitrales* (Volume XIX, 1990, pp. 149-196), https://doi.org/10.18356/e23828be-en-fr. [in French].
10. Hagenbuch, B. (2020, October 23). US Fishing Fleet in Bering Sea Rattled by Russian Military Exercises. *SeafoodSource*. https://www.seafoodsource.com/news/supply-trade/us-fishing-fleet-in-bering-sea-rattled-by-russian-military-exercises.
11. ICJ (1949). *Corfu Channel Case, Judgment of April 9th, 1949*: I.C.J. Reports 1949, p. 4.
12. ICJ (1985). *Continental Shelf (Libyan Arab Jamahiriya/Malta)*, Judgement, I.C.J. Reports 1985, 13.
13. India-Pakistan Agreement (1991). *Agreement on Advance Notice on Military Exercises, Manoeuvres and Troop Movements*, adopted 6 April 1991. https://treaties.un.org/doc/publication/unts/volume%201843/volume-1843-i-31420-english.pdf.
14. IMCO (1979). *World-Wide Navigational Warning Service*. Resolution A.419(XI), adopted 15 November 1979.
15. IMO (1991). *World-Wide Navigational Warning Service*. Resolution A.706(17), adopted 6 November 1991.
16. Karagiannis, S. (2004). L'Article 59 de la Convention des Nations Unies sur le Droit de la Mer (ou Les Mystères de la Nature Juridique de la Zone Économique Exclusive) [Article 59 of the United Nations Convention on the Law of the Sea (or Mysteries of the Legal Nature of the Exclusive Economic Zone]. *Revue Belge de Droit International*, 37(2), 325-418. [in French].
17. Konyshev, B. & Sergunin, A. (2014). Russia's Policies on the Territorial Disputes in the Arctic. *Journal of International Relations and Foreign Policy*, 2(1), 55-83.

18. Kunoy, B. (2017). La Zone Économique Exclusive (ZEE) [The Exclusive Economic Zone (EEZ)]. In Forteau, M. & Thouvenin, J.-M. (Eds.), *Traité de Droit International de la Mer* (pp. 384-399). Éditions A. Pedone. [in French].
19. Kwiatkowska, B. (1989). *The 200 Mile Exclusive Economic Zone in the New Law of the Sea* (Publications on Ocean Development, Volume 14). Martinus Nijhoff Publishers.
20. Madsen, S. (2020). *Testimony of Stephanie Madsen* (22 September 2020). Subcommittee on Security of the US Senate Committee on Commerce, Science, and Transportation. Retrieved from: https://meetings.npfmc.org/CommentReview/DownloadFile?p=ea62a3ee-a32b-4eec-bf3b-a12f68d35a83.pdf&fileName=200922%20Stephanie%20Madsen%20Testimony%20for%20U.S.%20Senate%20Commerce%20Committee%20Security%20Subcommittee.pdf.
21. Map 1 (1990). *Message from the President of the United States Transmitting the Agreement Between the United States of America and the Union of Soviet Socialist Republics on the Maritime Boundary, with Annex, Signed at Washington June 1, 1990.* Retrieved from: https://www.state.gov/wp-content/uploads/2020/02/US_Russia_1990.pdf.
22. NGA (no date). Maritime Safety Information, Navigational Warning Limits (Map) *(National Geospatial-Intelligence Agency).* Retrieved October 28, 2021 from: https://msi.nga.mil/api/publications/download?key=16920956/SFH00000/navwarnings.jpg&type=view.
23. NOAA (no date). *What Is the EEZ?* National Ocean Service. https://oceanservice.noaa.gov/facts/eez.html.
24. North Pacific Fishery Management Council (2020, October 20). *Russian Military Activity in the EEZ.* North Pacific Fishery Management Council. https://www.npfmc.org/russian-military-activity/.

25. Oxman, B. H. (2018). The Principle of Due Regard. In International Tribunal for the Law of the Sea, *The Contribution of the International Tribunal for the Law of the Sea to the Rule of Law: 1996-2016 / La Contribution du Tribunal International du Droit de la Mer à l'État de Droit: 1996-2016* (pp. 108-117). Brill Nijhoff.
26. Pedrozo, R. P. (2014). Military Activities in the Exclusive Economic Zone: East Asia Focus. *International Law Studies*, 90, 514-543.
27. Proelss, A. (2017). Exclusive Economic Zone. In Proelss, A. (Ed.), United Nations Convention on the Law of the Sea: A Commentary (pp. 408-586). Nomos Verlagsgesellschaft.
28. Quéneudec, J.-P. (1982). Zone Économique Exclusive et Forces Aéronavales [Exclusive Economic Zone and Air and Sea Powers]. In Académie de Droit International de La Haye (Ed.), *The Management of Humanity's Resources: The Law of the Sea* (Colloques/Workshop Series, pp. 319-324). Brill Nijhoff. [in French].
29. Rigaldies, F. (1997). La Zone Économique Exclusive dans la Pratique des États [The Exclusive Economic Zone in State Practice]. *Canadian Yearbook of International Law/Annuaire Canadien de Droit International*, 35, 3-56. [in French].
30. Rose, S. (1990). Naval Activity in the Exclusive Economic Zone—Troubled Waters Ahead? *Ocean Development and International Law*, 21(2), 123-145.
31. Ruskin, L. (2020, December 10). *Russian Intimidation of Bering Sea Fishermen Shows Gap in Arctic Investment, Sen. Sullivan Say*. KTOO. https://www.ktoo.org/2020/12/10/russian-intimidation-of-bering-sea-fishermen-shows-gap-in-arctic-investment-sullivan-says/.
32. Russia/Ukraine Agreement (2003). Договор между Российской Федерацией и Украиной о сотрудничестве в использовании Азовского моря и Керченского пролива [*Agreement between the Russian Federation and Ukraine on*

Cooperation in the Use of the Sea of Azov and the Kerch Strait]. Retrieved from: https://www.ecolex.org/details/treaty/agreement-between-the-russian-federation-and-the-ukraine-on-cooperation-in-the-use-of-the-sea-of-azov-and-the-strait-of-kerch-tre-149547/ [in Russian].
33. Rybolovstvo i Rybovodstvo (2020, September 3). Российские военные учения в Беринговом море встревожили американских промысловиков [Russian Military Exercises in the Bering Sea Alarmed American Fisherman]. *Rybolovstvo i Rybovodstvo.* https://www.magazine.fish/news/promyslovoe-rybolovstvo/rossiyskie_voennyy_flot_v_beringovom_more_vstrevozhil_amerikanskikh_promyslovikov/ [in Russian].
34. SOLAS (1974). International Convention for the Safety of Life at Sea, adopted 1 November 1974, entered into force 25 May 1980, as amended. Retrieved October 28, 2021, from: http://tuapseport.ru/Eng/Solas/solas_chIV_C.htm#Reg_12.
35. Soluri, E. A. (1998). Promulgation of Navigational Warnings under the Global Maritime Distress and Safety System. *International Hydrographic Review*, LXXV(2), 15-25.
36. State Duma (2002). Постановление Государственной Думы Федерального Собрания РФ от 14 июня 2002 г. No 2880-III ГД *"О последствиях применения Соглашения между Союзом Советских Социалистических Республик и Соединёнными Штатами Америки о линии разграничения морских пространств 1990 года для национальных интересов Российской Федерации"* [Resolution № 2880-III G.D *On the Implications of the Provisional Implementation of the Agreement Between the Union of Soviet Socialist Republics and the United States of America on the Line of Demarcation of Maritime Spaces of 1990 for National Interests of the Russian Federation*], 14 June 2002. [in Russian].
37. Sukhankin, S. (2020). The Northeastern Dimension of Russia's 'Ocean Shield 2020' Naval Exercises (Part One). *Eurasia Daily Monitor*, 17(125). *The Jamestown Foundation:*

Global Research & Analysis. Retrieved October 29, 2021 from: https://jamestown.org/program/the-northeastern-dimension-of-russias-ocean-shield-2020-naval-exercises-part-one/.
38. The Associated Press (2020, August 30). Over 50 Warships Were Involved in Russian Navy Exercises that Surprised Alaska Trawlers. *Alaska Public Media.* https://www.alaskapublic.org/2020/08/30/over-50-warships-were-involved-in-russian-navy-exercises-that-surprised-alaskan-trawlers/.
39. Tsarev, V. F. (1988). Peaceful Uses of the Seas: Principles and Complexities. *Marine Policy*, 12(2), 153-159.
40. United Nations Convention on the Law of the Sea, 10 December 1982, https://www.un.org/depts/los/convention_agreements/texts/unclos/unclos_e.pdf.
41. United Nations Secretariat (1983). *Document A/CONF.62/WS/37 and ADD.1-2*. In *United Nations*, Official Record of the Third United Nations Conference on the law of the Sea, Volume XVII (Plenary Meetings, Summary Records and Verbatim Records, as well as Documents of the Conference, Resumed Session and Final Part Eleventh Session and Conclusion), 240-244. Available at: https://legal.un.org/diplomaticconferences/1973_los/docs/english/vol_17/a_conf62_ws_37_and_add1_2.pdf.
42. US Coast Guard (2018). *Termination of U.S. Coast Guard Rebroadcast of HYDROLANT and HYDROPAC Information*, 8 August 2018 (Federal Register, 83(153), 39109). Retrieved from: https://www.govinfo.gov/content/pkg/FR-2018-08-08/pdf/2018-16954.pdf.
43. US-Russia Convention (1867). *Treaty Concerning the Cession of the Russian Possessions in North America by His Majesty the Emperor of All the Russias to the United States of America*, concluded 30 March 1867, ratified by the United States 28 May 1867, exchanged 20 June 1867, proclaimed 20 June 1867. Available at: https://tile.loc.gov/storage-ser

vices/service/gdc/dcmsia-books/tr/ea/ty/co/nc/er/ni/ng/00/un/it/treatyconcerning00unit/treatyconcerning00unit.pdf.
44. US/USSR Agreement (1990). *Agreement Between the United States of America and the Union of Soviet Socialist Republics on Maritime Boundary*, adopted 1 June 1990. Available at: https://www.un.org/depts/los/LEGISLATIONANDTREATIES/PDFFILES/TREATIES/USA-RUS1990MB.PDF.
45. Vienna Convention (1969). *Vienna Convention on the Law of Treaties*, adopted 23 May 1969, entered into force 27 January 1980. https://legal.un.org/ilc/texts/instruments/english/conventions/1_1_1969.pdf.

ASSESSING CHINA'S SECURITIZATION OF ARCTIC CLIMATE CHANGE AND ENERGY
Yue Wang & Liling Xu

Abstract

China has been actively involved in Arctic affairs, facing both opportunities and challenges brought by accelerated climate change in the Arctic. China also shows increasing security concerns in the Arctic, which is manifested in the incorporation of the polar regions in "China's National Security Law" in 2015 and implied in the extensive connections between China and the Arctic in "China's Arctic Policy" in 2018. However, how the Arctic and China's national security have been connected and circulated in the wider Chinese discourses, and whether China has taken or can take exceptional measures to successfully securitize the Arctic are still unclear. This chapter draws on Copenhagen School's securitization theory to analyze China's securitization of Arctic climate change and Arctic energy affairs, which are the most relevant Arctic issues to China and can reflect China's efforts to address the "Arctic paradox" (De Botselier, López Piqueres, & Schunz, 2018). By examining 'speech acts' in Chinese policy documents, political speeches, scholarly publications, media coverages, and Chinese energy enterprises' press releases and documents, we argue that China's securitization of Arctic climate change and energy affairs is still shown as ongoing securitizing moves that are far from successful securitization with exceptional measures beyond normal politics. In China's securitizing moves of Arctic climate change and energy affairs, the securitizing actor (the state) adopts relatively ambiguous discourses linking the Arctic and China's national security, compared to those of functional actors (Chinese academia, mass media and energy enterprises). We also notice that both threats and potential benefits trigger China's securitizing moves of Arctic energy affairs, and it seems benefits play a more critical role, which indicates a counterfactual logic. By attending to the role of and interactions among the securitizing actor and the functional actors in China's securitizing moves of climate change and energy in the Arctic, this chapter attempts to add nuances to China's efforts in securitizing Arctic affairs and to shed light on the understanding of 'securitization' in the Chinese context.

Keywords: Copenhagen School of securitization; securitization of the Arctic; China; climate change; energy security

Introduction

China has been actively involved in Arctic affairs, facing both opportunities and challenges brought by accelerated climate change in the Arctic. China's Arctic policies and practices have been underpinned by its wide interests in Arctic scientific research, resource exploration and development, Arctic shipping routes with growing navigability, and so forth (Andersson, 2021; Dodds & Nuttall, 2015; Hong, 2020; Lu & Zhang, 2016). Among these interests, China has shown increasing security concerns over the socio-economic impact of Arctic climate change on China and the security of Chinese individuals, facilities, and investments in the region. Polar regions[1] have been incorporated into China's national security agenda in Article 32 of "China's National Security Law", stating that China persists in "preserving the security of our nation's activities and assets in outer space, seabed areas and polar regions, and other interests" (Xinhua News Agency, 2015). Besides, China's first-ever published Arctic White Paper - "China's Arctic Policy", defined China as a "near-Arctic state"[2] (近北极国家) and addressed extensive connections between the Arctic and China in terms of geography, climate system, ecological environment, and economic interests (State Council Information Office of the People's Republic of China (the PRC), 2018), which also has security indications as the following parts demonstrate. However, how the Arctic and China's national security have been connected and circulated in the wider Chinese discourses, and whether China has taken or can take exceptional measures beyond general rules or normal politics to successfully securitize the Arctic are still unclear.

To answer these questions, this chapter draws on the Copenhagen School's securitization theory to examine China's securitization of the Arctic in relation to climate change and energy. Climate change and energy security are of increasing importance to China because of their significant impact on China's economic prosperity and national security (Nyman & Zeng, 2016). Besides, the management of the growing tension between energy exploitation and addressing climate change is of critical importance to demonstrate China's role in dealing with these issues globally. This tension has become ever more prominent in the Arctic considering the urgent need to address the 'Arctic paradox' - "the tradeoff between pursuing the economic opportunities arising from an increasingly ice-free Arctic and preventing environmental degradation in a region of central importance for the global climate" (De Botselier, López Piqueres, & Schunz, 2018, p.3). In this context, China has become a critical actor shaping and being shaped by the geophysical transformation and geopolitical changes in the Arctic, including the security dynamics.

The Copenhagen School of international relations emerged in the late 1980s, expanded the 'security' concept to military, political, societal, economic, and environmental security sectors, not merely limited to the traditional military security sector (Buzan, Waever, & de Wilde, 1998), and introduced the key concept of "securitization". Securitization refers to the process where securitizing actors construct that a valuable referent object is under existential threats through discursive practices- the so-called 'speech acts'- and calls for exceptional measures beyond normal politics (Buzan & Hansen, 2009; Buzan, Waever, & de Wilde, 1998). Securitization theory has been widely applied in the analysis of interstate relations in the Arctic (Åtland, 2008; Dodds & Nuttall, 2015), Arctic governance (Greaves & Pomerants, 2017; Jacobsen & Strandsbjerg, 2017), and the shift of the 'Arctic security' concept from military and state sovereignty towards a more comprehensive definition incorporating environmental, economic, human, health and cultural dimensions (Cambou & Hossain, 2019; Heininen, Exner-Pirot & Barnes, 2019; Jacobsen & Herrmann, 2017). However, existing studies mainly focus on the securitization practices of Arctic states, while China and other non-Arctic states and organizations have not received enough attention with merely few exceptions (Deng, 2020; Lanteigne, 2015; Wang, 2013). These studies have applied the securitization theory to analyze China's Arctic engagement in general but the detailed securitization dynamics within China have not been adequately addressed. While analytically useful, the Copenhagen School's approach was largely informed by the experiences of Western liberal democracies. This chapter explores China's efforts in the securitization of the Arctic, which attempts to add nuances to China's efforts in securitizing Arctic affairs and to shed light on the understanding of securitization dynamics in the Chinese context.

Following the call on a more contextualized analysis to approach securitization, especially in a non-Western context (Freeman, 2010; Nyman & Zeng, 2016; Zhang, 2010), this chapter aims to delve into the process of associating the Arctic and China's national security in climate change and energy security sectors. By engaging with China's securitizing moves of Arctic climate change and Arctic energy affairs from both traditional and non-traditional security perspectives, we found that they are still ongoing processes, far from being successful securitization with exceptional measures beyond normal politics. We argue that in China's securitizing moves of Arctic climate change and energy affairs, the securitizing actor (the state) adopts relatively ambiguous discourses linking the Arctic and China's national security, compared to those of functional actors (Chinese academia, mass media and energy enterprises). We also notice that both threats and potential benefits trigger China's securitizing moves of Arctic energy affairs, and it seems benefits play a more important role. This indicates a counterfactual logic: China's energy supply and the sustainability of its national energy system are under threat but not because of Arctic energy affairs. Instead, the situations of the referent objects would worsen if China does not act on Arctic energy affairs timely and seriously.

The chapter unfolds in the following four sections. First, it outlines the development of the Copenhagen School's securitization theory and the Arctic securitization trajectory. The subsequent two sections analyze China's securitizing moves of Arctic climate change and energy affairs by examining 'speech acts' in Chinese policy documents, political speeches, scholarly publications, media coverages, and Chinese energy enterprises' press releases and documents. In this process, the specific referent objects, securitizing actors, and functional actors in each securitizing move are identified, and their roles are analyzed accordingly. The concluding section reflects on the application of the Copenhagen School's securitization theory on China's securitizing moves of the Arctic. It puts forward further questions to consider, such as whether counterfactual logic is a more general tendency in China's securitizing moves of international affairs.

Securitization theory and the Arctic securitization trajectory
International security studies rose to prominence after World War II (Miller, 2001) and continued to develop during the Cold War. In this period, international security studies were literally strategic studies, focusing on military threats to the state and the use of force (Buzan & Hansen, 2017). Afterwards, the dominant focus on military security got challenged by Cold War peace research, the occurrence of oil crises of the 1970s, and post-Cold War critical approaches (Buzan & Hansen, 2009), and non-military sectors were introduced when understanding the concept of 'security'. In this context, the Copenhagen School of international relations emerged and grew in the late 1980s and expanded the 'security' concept to military, political, societal, economic, and environmental security sectors (Buzan, Waever, & de Wilde, 1998). The Copenhagen School also introduced a key concept – *securitization* (Buzan, Waever, & de Wilde, 1998; Waever, 1995), which refers to a process by which a given issue becomes a security issue. Securitization is a process of constructing an urgent existential threat to a *referent object*, and such a threat calls for exceptional measures beyond the general rules or above politics (Buzan & Hansen, 2017; Buzan, Waever, & de Wilde, 1998). "Political leaders, bureaucracies, governments, lobbyists, and pressure groups" are common *securitizing actors* (Buzan, Waever,

& de Wilde, 1998, p. 40) that can construct a referent object being existentially threatened in the discourses, namely, starting a *securitizing move*. In general, a state has concrete rules to define who can represent it. For example, governments, bureaucracies, and political leaders of the current government can usually speak on behalf of the state.

A securitizing move is the premise of a successful securitization, and a securitization process is embodied as speech acts mainly performed by securitizing actors. As "an operative method" (Wæver, 2015, p. 122), speech act theory is the foundation of securitization theory. The core idea of speech act theory is "that people do things by talking, that they perform different kinds of acts by speaking" (Vuori, 2016, p. 4). A security speech act is "by saying 'security'", securitizing actors "declare[s] an emergency condition, thus claiming a right to use whatever means are necessary to block a threatening development" (Buzan & Hansen, 2009, pp. 33-34). The securitization dynamics is also under the influence of different *functional actors*. Unlike securitizing actors, functional actors are not in the position to move a certain issue beyond the general rules (i.e., do not have the power to do so). However, they can significantly affect the dynamics of a securitizing move. According to Eroukhmanoff (2018), academia, media, and non-governmental organizations (NGOs) are common functional actors. A securitizing move will turn to a successful securitization only when a speech act becomes "a combination of language and society" (Buzan, Waever, & de Wilde, 1998, p. 32). Namely, internally, the speech needs to follow "the grammar of security" (Buzan, Waever, & de Wilde, 1998, p. 33); externally, the society needs to "authorize[s] and recognize[s] that speech" (Buzan, Waever, & de Wilde, 1998, p. 32), that is, the acceptance of an audience (Buzan, Waever, & de Wilde, 1998, p. 25). From the Copenhagen School's securitization perspective, the Arctic has experienced the "securitization - de-securitization - re-securitization" process (Deng, 2020, p. 3). During the Cold War, potential military conflicts between the Soviet Union and the United States

(US) in the circumpolar north securitized the Arctic in both discursive and practical dimensions. The Arctic region was seen as a sensitive military theatre in which political, economic, cultural and other interests were subordinated to national security interests (Åtland, 2008, p. 290). The former President of the Soviet Union *Mikhail Gorbachev* in 1987 called out that "let the North of the globe, the Arctic, become a zone of peace. Let the North Pole be a pole of peace" (known as 'Gorbachev's Murmansk speech') (Gorbachev, 1987). Following that, the Arctic was gradually entering into the stage of de-securitization in the post-Cold War era. 'De-securitization' here refers to the shift from "the emergency mode" to "the normal bargaining process of the political sphere" (Buzan, Waever, & de Wilde, 1998, p. 4). In other words, sovereignty disputes in the Arctic were generally contained or localized (Jacobsen & Strandsbjerg, 2017), the strategic value of the Arctic as the buffer zone between the superpowers was diminished (Lanteigne, 2015, p. 151), and a wide range of international and regional cooperation arrangements in the Arctic were generated (Åtland, 2008). In 1996, the Arctic Council, the leading intergovernmental forum of Arctic affairs, was established. It self-consciously identified eight Arctic States Members and six Indigenous peoples' organizations as Permanent Participants (Arctic Council, no year). The Arctic Council also accepts observer's applications from other stakeholders outside the Arctic and aims to create a circumpolar platform for collaboration, and constantly insists that traditional security affairs are out of its mandate (Arctic Council, no year).

In the 21st century, due to the acceleration of climate change, a series of new changes in the Arctic has occurred, such as the growing navigability of the Arctic shipping routes and the prospect of enormous oil and gas potentials, which have triggered global interests in the Arctic (Lanteigne, 2015, p. 151). The prospects of the Arctic, unsettled territorial disputes between Arctic states, rising military presence in the Arctic, and growing involvements of non-Arctic states, such as China, have raised increasing concerns over Arctic security.

There is an increasingly popular standpoint: the Arctic has been portrayed as returning back to geopolitical conflicts, and the future of the Arctic would be characterized by competition and increasing tensions and even military threats and conflicts, which were permeated throughout the Cold War (for example, Financial Times, 2007; Gross, 2020; Luhn, 2020; Saxena, 2020). All these are the signs of re-securitization of the Arctic. However, it should be noted that this 're-securitization' tendency in the Arctic mainly stays at a discursive level, rather than actual practical attempts shown in the previous securitization during the Cold War (Jacobsen & Strandsbjerg, 2017, p. 20). Additionally, the Arctic conflict narrative is more popular among the players outside the Arctic, particularly outside the European Arctic region. In fact, the narrative from the Arctic prefers to believe there is low conflict potential in the Arctic (for example, Käpylä & Mikkola, 2013; Olesen, 2014; Rosamond, 2011; Young, 2011).

In spite of the debate over the conflict potential in the Arctic, the Arctic has been on a re-securitization trajectory (Gricius, 2021), at least in a narrative sense, and more players are taking part in this re-securitization process, including China. Drawing on the Copenhagen School's securitization theory and keeping China's social and political systems in mind, this chapter analyzes the role of China in the re-securitization of the Arctic from both perspectives of traditional security and non-traditional security. The Copenhagen School's securitization theory has a strong "Western-centric nature" (Nyman & Zeng, 2016, p. 302), and most of the existing literature focuses on studying the securitization practices in "more or less [Western] democratic" (Vuori, 2008, p. 65) political systems where the wide acceptance of the audience, namely, the population, is necessary for a successful securitization. Thus, its usefulness in non-Western contexts has been questioned. However, the audience does not always need to be the "entire population" (Hansen, 2000, p. 289) or the "general public" (Vuori, 2008, p. 72) or "citizenry" (Waever, 2003, p. 11), the audience in the process of securitization could be restricted to "the power elite" (Hansen, 2000, p. 289; Vuori, 2008, p.

72) or "a group of fundamentalists" (Vuori, 2008, p. 72) in the countries with non-Western social and political systems. Also, some researchers, such as Wilkinson (2007) with the empirical study of Kyrgyzstan and Vuori (2008 and 2011) with the empirical study of China, have justified that the securitization theory can still be adopted in non-Western political systems, but more attention needs to be paid to social and political contexts where the securitization in question is happening.

Arctic climate change and China's national security

The Arctic has warmed "three times"[3] faster than the world as a whole over the past five decades (Arctic Monitoring & Assessment Programme, 2021), and climate change has become one of the key drivers of changes in Arctic physical and geopolitical landscapes. As Arctic Sea ice melts, Arctic shipping routes and resource extraction become increasingly feasible, while the Arctic States' maritime and coastal boundaries disputes are still unsolved. It also attracts actors outside the region, including China, who has long noticed that Arctic climate change is of its economic, environmental, and scientific interests and has increasingly engaged in Arctic affairs.

"Climate security" refers to "how climate change and security are interlinked in a specific context, as the process legitimizes and delegitimizes actions, and empowers and disempowers actors" (Trombetta, 2019, p. 102). Recent Chinese political and academic discourses on Arctic affairs illustrate an emerging security logic and reasoning that links Arctic climate change and China's increasingly active engagement. In other words, securitizing moves of Arctic climate change are ongoing in China, which has been used to explain and legitimize China's increased involvement in Arctic economic, scientific, governance and strategic affairs. In the process of securitizing the Arctic, China, the state, is the securitizing actor who raises the awareness of Arctic climate change among domestic audiences and responds to international suspicions and concerns over China's engagement (for example, Brady, 2017; Jakobson, 2015; Wishnick,

2019). As the following section illustrates, China's official discourses depict both China and the Arctic as referent objects facing security threats from climate change. Constructing the state itself as a referent object enables China to justify its identities as a "near-Arctic state" and a "stakeholder" in the region and the increasing Chinese involvement in the Arctic. Portraying the Arctic as a referent object creates space for China to construct itself as a responsible and cooperative contributor to the vulnerable Arctic, which in turn further justifies its increasing participation in Arctic affairs. Chinese academia and influential mass media are the main functional actors that serve policymaking and bring Arctic climate change and China's Arctic activities to the public attention. They portray China as the referent object facing wide existential threats from Arctic climate change from the perspectives of traditional security (such as military and political security) and non-traditional security (such as economic security, climate security, ecological security, and so forth). The divergent framings of referent objects are relevant to different targeted audiences and the border context of China's securitization of climate change. This section begins with an overview of the progress of China's incorporation of global climate change into its national security agenda before delving into China's securitizing moves of Arctic climate change.

Global climate change and China's national security
Global climate change has long been identified as a development issue rather than a security issue in China (Brauch & Scheffran, 2012; Nyman & Zeng, 2016; Trombetta, 2019; Zhang, 2010). This is due to the priority of economic development in China's national agenda, China's distinct perceptions of security threats, and its concerns over restrictions, and interference of other international actors resulting from securitizing climate change (Bo, 2016; Jakobson, 2015; Nyman & Zeng, 2016; Sahu, 2021; Yu & Xie, 2015). Initial discussions over the connections between climate change and national security emerged in Chinese academic publications in the 2010s (for exam-

ple, Zhang 2010; Zhang, W. M., 2017). Such connections with climate change gradually prevailed in Chinese official documents during this period. One prominent example is the evolving discourses about the linkages between climate change and China's national security in "National Assessment Report on Climate Change", an authoritative report series compiled and published by the Ministry of Science and Technology, China Meteorological Administration and Chinese Academy of Sciences in 2006, 2011 and 2015. Compared with the reports in 2006 and 2011 that attended to the economic and social impact of climate change, the most recent report in 2015 explicitly articulated the relationship between climate change and China's national security that "climate change is related to China's economic security, energy security, ecological security and food security" in the preface (The Third National Assessment Report on Climate Change Committee, 2015, p. 1). Moreover, the third report noticeably included a separate section about polar regions pertaining to the influence of Arctic ice melting on China's sea-level rise and extreme weathers (The Third National Assessment Report on Climate Change Committee, 2015, p. 165). It is evident that the connections between climate change and China's national security have been gradually acknowledged in Chinese academic publications and official discourses.

Chinese academia plays a role as a functional actor in the securitization of global climate change. Generally speaking, Chinese scholars influence foreign policy from bottom to top as an "epistemic community" providing insightful information to policy makers to directly influences China's foreign policy, or as a 'mirror' to reflect Chinese foreign policy orientations and even domestic political directions (Feng, He, & Yan, 2019, pp. 9,13). An "epistemic community", according to *Peter Haas,* is "a network of professionals with recognized expertise and competence in a particular domain and an authoritative claim to policy-relevant knowledge within that domain or issue-area" (Haas, 1992, p. 3). One avenue for Chinese academia to provide advice is through research projects initiated by government agencies. In 2012, Chinese scholars in International Relations from several renowned research institutions and universities collaboratively participated in a research project- "Key Technology Research on Climate Change and National Security Strategy" under "the 'Twelfth Five-Year' National Science and Technology Support Program Project" announced by the Ministry of Science and Technology of the PRC. The project was led by *Zhang Haibin*, a professor from the School of International Studies of Peking University, who published the first book systematically elaborating the impact of climate change on China's national security (Zhang, 2010). The project attended to climate change issues within and outside the Chinese territories, including regions alongside the China 'Belt and Road Initiative' (the BRI), the Arctic, Brazil, Mexico, and so forth (School of International Studies, Peking University, 2016). By extending the focus from domestic areas to global regions, this project was set to advice the state in international climate negotiations primarily under the United Nations Framework Convention on Climate Change (UNFCCC) (School of International Studies, Peking University, 2012), playing the role of the "epistemic community" to inform China's diplomacy practices. Some consultation reports were approved by Chinese top political leaders, such as President *Xi Jinping*, Vice Premier *Zhang Gaoli*, and the research team gained recognition from National Development and Reform Commission, Ministry of Foreign Affairs, and the then Ministry of Environmental Protection (replaced by Ministry of Ecology and Environment since 2018). They also contributed to drafting an important chapter on climate security in one of the United Nations Panel on Climate Change assessment reports (School of International Studies, Peking University, 2016).

Arctic climate change and China's national security

China's securitization of climate change in the Arctic was unfolded in the extensive context of addressing global climate change. The Copenhagen School of securitization constructs certain referent objects under existential threats through speech acts. Chinese mass media is an influential functional actor in establishing the linkages between Arctic climate change and China's security, especially in their coverage of China's Arctic scientific research. China's Arctic research activities mainly focus on climate and environmental change issues (Heggelund & Han, 2019, p. 142), aiming to understand the impact of Arctic climate change on China. Media coverage frames more frequent extreme weather and sea-level rise brought by climate change as existential threats to the socio-economic security of China and Chinese people's safety. In reports of China's first Arctic scientific expedition, *People's Daily (人民日报)* and *Guangming Daily (光明日报)*, two influential Chinese state-affiliated newspapers, articulated that one major scientific question was "the Arctic's role in global change and its impact on China's climate" (Li, 2001; Ren, 1999). The media coverage of the second Arctic scientific expedition took a further step to address the socio-economic connections between Arctic climate change and China. According to *People's Daily*, "changes in the Arctic also have a significant impact on China's climate and environment. Understanding these issues is a major issue related to China's national economy and people's livelihood" (Xiang, 2003). In the latest coverage of China's 12th scientific expedition in 2021, *Xinhua News Agency (新华社)* made it clear that "the natural conditions and changes in the Arctic have a direct impact on China's climate system and ecological environment, and in turn are related to China's economic interests in the fields of agriculture, forestry, fisheries, and oceans" (Wang & Zhang, 2021). A more explicit statement of the possible security threats can be found in an interview on China *Meteorological News (中国气象报)* with *Xiao Dong*, a researcher in Chinese Academy of Meteorological Sciences. Xiao called for actions to "prevent threats to the lives and property of Chinese from extreme weather and climate events caused by the warming Arctic" (Wang, M. L., 2020).

While Chinese mass media plays a critical role in disseminating the impacts of Arctic climate change on China from the economy, ecology and society perspectives, Chinese scholars in International Relations and International Law lead the securitizing move of Arctic climate change so as to raise the Arctic in China's political agenda since the first decade of the 21st Century. Russian flag-planting on the seabed of the Arctic Ocean in 2007 and the accompanying international responses marked the beginning of this process. These Chinese scholars also draw on scientific evidence to highlight the impact of Arctic climate change on China's national security from various aspects. For example, some earlier discussions noticed the impact of Arctic ice melting on China's national security from the non-traditional security perspective, including China's ecological security, food security and climate driven insecurities in coastal areas (Lu, 2010, p. 297; Xia, 2011, p. 130; Zhang, 2010, p. 62), which was further expanded to other non-traditional security sectors, such as military and political security (Sun & Wu, 2016, p. 74; Wang, 2013, p. 114). By constructing these concerns as security issues, Chinese academia acts as a functional actor who has significantly moved up Arctic issues in China's foreign policy agenda.

Chinese media and academia frame China (the state and Chinese people's livelihood) as a referent object under various existential threats imposed by Arctic climate change. By contrast, Chinese official discourses refer to both the Arctic and China as referent objects and deliberate security threats in a less straightforward way. There was no shortage of descriptions framing China as the referent object of Arctic climate change. For example, at the Third Arctic Circle Assembly in 2015 (Reykjavik, Iceland), *Zhang Ming*, the then Vice Foreign Minister, delivered a keynote speech titled "China's Contribution: Respect, Cooperation and Win-win". *Zhang* highlighted the impact of Arctic climate change on China's climate, environment, agriculture, shipping, trade, and socio-economic development to portray China as 'an important stakeholder' (Ministry of Foreign Affairs of the PRC, 2015). China's Arctic White Paper declared that "the natural conditions of the Arctic and their changes have a direct impact on China's climate system and ecological environment, and, in turn, on its economic interests in agriculture, forestry, fishery, marine industry and other sectors" (State Council Information Office of the PRC, 2018). These discourses clearly underscore various connections between China and Arctic climate change from the non-traditional security perspective, whereas the linkage to the traditional military security is largely missing. This is understandable given the fact that military discourses might be incompatible with the aim of the White Paper, which according to *Zhang Xia*, the then director of Polar Strategy Research Office of the Polar Research Institute of China (PRIC), seeks to clarify China's position and goals on Arctic affairs and eliminate international suspicions over China's propositions (China News Service, 2018).

Meanwhile, Chinese official discourses have adopted security-related expressions to construct the Arctic as the other referent object under threats of climate change and the accompanying commercial activities. For example, the state often shows security concerns over the vulnerable Arctic ecosystems, the livelihoods of local inhabitants and indigenous communities in the Arctic (for example, Ministry of Foreign Affairs of the PRC, 2017; Ministry of Foreign Affairs of the PRC, 2019), as the "indicator of global climate change" (Ministry of Foreign Affairs of the PRC, 2015). In China's Arctic White Paper, the state further pinpointed that there are "various traditional and non-traditional security threats" in the Arctic, such as potential security threats to "the ecological environment of the Arctic" caused by the increasing commercial activities in the Arctic (State Council Information Office of the PRC, 2018). When constructing the Arctic as one referent object, the state also constructs itself as a "responsible contributor" (Chinese Antarctic Center of Surveying and Mapping, Wuhan University) to mitigate the security risks in the vulnerable Arctic, such as emission reduction, scientific knowledge contribution, and other efforts through global, regional, multilateral and bilateral cooperation. Thus, constructing the Arctic region as the other referent object can highlight its identity as a "responsible contributor" to the Arctic to mitigate international suspicions and, similar to the efforts to securitize China itself under threats of Arctic climate change, to justify its increasing participation in Arctic affairs.

All in all, by analyzing Chinese scholarly, media and official discourses, it is evident that China has constructed its national security under threats due to Arctic climate change via speech acts. However, securitizing Arctic climate change is still an ongoing securitizing move in China rather than a successful securitization, as so far there have been only ambiguous speech acts, which are far from exceptional measures beyond normal politics. In this securitizing move, the state is the securitizing actor, and the mass media and academia take the role of key functional actors. The state constructs both China (the state and Chinese people's livelihood) and the Arctic as referent objects under threats due to Arctic climate change, targeting domestic and international audiences. Chinese mass media and academia are the main functional actors. They construct Arctic climate change as an existential threat to the state and Chinese people's livelihood from both traditional and non-traditional security perspectives, raising the awareness of the impact of Arctic climate change among the general public and policymakers. Despite different approaches and audiences, these speech acts unanimously serve to legitimize China's participation in Arctic affairs, facilitate international cooperation in the Arctic region, and provide an avenue for more active participation in Arctic governance (Dai, 2021, p. 86; Doshi, Dale-Huang, & Zhang, 2021, p. 14).

Arctic energy resources and China's energy security
Energy security is a key element of China's national security, consisting of both traditional and non-traditional security concerns (China's Public Communication Office of National Security, 2021). According to an assessment by the United States Geological Survey (USGS), energy potentials in the Arctic are significantly rich (USGS, 2008). The Arctic may hold approximately 22 percent of the planet's technically recoverable but undiscovered oil and gas resources. Wide interests from international actors are triggered by the

newly-found abundant energy potentials and the increasing availability of these energy resources in the context of the accelerated climate change in the Arctic. China has been paying more attention to Arctic energy resources gradually due to its rapidly growing domestic energy demand (Hsiung, 2016; Sun & Ma, 2018) and its systematic energy transition to carbon neutrality (Shanghai Institutes for International Studies, 2021; Spivak, 2021). These two reasons for China's growing interests in Arctic energy resources are linked to traditional energy security and non-traditional energy security, respectively. On the one hand, traditional energy security analysts focus on energy supply, its impact on (traditional) national security (for example, "maintaining the existence of the state") (Cornell, 2009, p. 64) and other strategic significance of energy resources (Mulligan, 2010; Nyman & Zeng, 2016), which is still the mainstream in energy security studies. On the other hand, emerging non-traditional energy security studies adopt "a human security lens", attending to the "well-being of states and societies" as well as "the linkage between energy security, climate change, health, environmental degradation, and energy sustainability" (Caballero-Anthony & Putra, 2012, p. 3). Following that, this section analyzes China and the securitization of the Arctic from the perspectives of traditional energy security and non-traditional energy security, respectively.

Arctic energy resources and China's traditional energy security
China has been the largest oil and gas importer in the world (US International Trade Administration, 2021). Based on the International Energy Agency (IEA), China has been a net energy importer since 1997, and its consumption of crude oil and natural gas, even coal, is heavily dependent on imports (IEA, no year). A stable energy supply is a key to ensuring the development of the world's second-largest economy. The energy security concern has been raised and spread quickly in China (Ellinas, 2020; Wang, 2021) due to the growing domestic energy demand (Sandkelf, 2004; Yang, Sun & Xin, 2015; Zhang, 2013) and the heavy reliance on importing foreign energy resources (Chen, 2012; Kiesow, 2004; Zhang & Li, 2010).

As the significance of Arctic oil and gas resources stands out, Chinese academia, major energy enterprises, and influential mass media play a role as functional actors to facilitate the securitizing move of Arctic energy affairs in China. Chinese academia acts as a critical functional actor who seeks to offer policy advice regarding Arctic energy resources to the state. For instance, some Chinese scholars strongly advocated that Arctic energy resources are a key source of China's energy supply and can contribute to the diversification of its energy supply, which is pivotal for China's economic development, social stability and national security (Lei & Yin, 2014; Liu & Hu, 2016; Pan, 2014; Sun & Wu, 2016; Xiao, 2016; Yang et al., 2013; Yang & Guo, 2017; Yang, Sun & Xin, 2015; Zhang & Li, 2010). Russia plays a dominant role in the Arctic hydrocarbons (more than 53 percent of crude oil reserves and around 95 percent of natural gas are in the Russian territory) (Devyatkin, 2018; Gautier et al., 2009). The close Sino-Russian relationship, expected to be strengthened further (Radin et al., 2021), guarantees China's stable energy supplies from the Arctic. Besides that, some Chinese scholars, such as *Lei* and *Yin* (Lei & Yin, 2014) and *Pan* (Pan, 2014), pinpointed that China's energy security also benefits from the emerging Arctic shipping routes, which provide safer and more cost-effective transportation of Arctic energy resources, compared to the traditional energy shipping routes, such as the Strait of Malacca and the Suez Canal, that are geopolitically sensitive and vulnerable to pirate attacks.

As a functional actor in China's securitizing moves of Arctic energy affairs, some Chinese academic opinions have been well noticed by the securitizing actor (the state). For example, *Jia* (Jia, 2017) called on the state to incorporate the Arctic energy resources into its overseas oil and gas development strategy and more actively march in exploring and developing Arctic energy resources without any delay. Interestingly, this article was reprinted by the then Ministry of Land and Resources of the PRC (replaced by the Ministry of Natural Resources of the PRC since 2018) on the same day when this article got published on July 14, 2017. *Feng, He,* and *Yan* proposed a well-established analytical framework on the role of Chinese scholars in

China's foreign policymaking (Feng, He, & Yan, 2019). However, drawing on this framework, it is still unclear whether *Jia*'s (Jia, 2017) understanding of Arctic energy resources directly informed China's foreign policy or whether it was a policy signal "before new policies or policy changes are formalized" (Feng, He, & Yan, 2019, p. 4). However, the immediate reprinting action indicates the close relationship between the state as the securitizing actor and Chinese academia as a functional actor.

Although seeking economic interests is an important motivation for China's major energy enterprises to participate in Arctic energy affairs (Sørensen & Klimenko, 2017, p. 12), these enterprises also attend to the security and other strategic significance of Arctic energy resources. For instance, the state-owned and China's largest oil and gas enterprise, China National Petroleum Corporation (CNPC), underscored that the successful operation of the Yamal Liquefied Natural Gas (LNG) project with China's key involvement incorporated the Arctic region into China's BRI, in particular, strongly promoted the development of the emerging Polar Silk Road (PSR) as a new expansion of China's BRI (CNPC, 2017). Yamal LNG project is a mega energy project located on the Yamal Peninsula in Russia with a joint venture of NOVATEK (Russia), TOTAL (France), CNPC (China), and Silk Road Fund (China), encompassing natural gas production, liquefaction and shipping (TotalEnergies, no year). Stable and sufficient LNG shipped from the Yamal LNG project to China can facilitate national economic development and strengthen national energy security in China (CNPC, 2017).

CNPC also argued that the successful operation of the Yamal LNG project in which China has been actively involved symbolizes promising progress of China's "march to Arctic energy resources" (An et al., 2018). Additionally, CNPC reprinted some journal articles focusing on Arctic energy and energy security, such as *Wang*'s article "Oil and Gas Resources in the Arctic" (Wang, D. R., 2020; reprinted in CNPC, 2020). In this article, *Wang* (Wang, D. R., 2020) called the state to pay close attention to the strategic opportunities generated by Arctic energy resources. For example, Arctic energy resources can help the state cope with its domestic energy crisis and enhance energy security. Besides CNPC, another key state-owned energy enterprise - China Petroleum & Chemical Corporation (Sinope) - also shows its concern about energy security issues related to Arctic energy resources, although it has not been directly involved in major Arctic energy projects. For instance, *Lei* and *Yin* (Lei & Yin, 2014), from the Sinope Exploration and Production Research Centre, firmly highlighted that Chinese energy enterprises must put national energy security in the first place when participating in the exploration and development of Arctic energy resources.

Moreover, China's influential mass media, such as *People's Daily, Guangming Daily, Xinhua News Agency, Reference News* （参考消息） and *Beijing Youth Daily* （北京青年报）, share closely similar arguments with Chinese academia and China's major energy enterprises regarding the impacts of Arctic energy resources on China's energy security. The Yamal LNG project is also the core of their media reports. The most common arguments are as follows: the active involvement in exploring and developing Arctic energy resources is significant for China to expand energy reserves (Lin, 2016), diversify and stabilize energy supply (Luo, 2018; Ran, 2018), ensure energy security or national security in general (Jiang, 2018; Wu & Qu, 2017; Xu, 2018; Zhang, X. D., 2017), improve discursive power in international energy governance (Wu & Qu, 2017), and prompt the development of the emerging PSR or the BRI in general (Guan et al., 2018; Li, 2018; Luo, 2018; Zhang, Y., 2017). Evidently, the security and other strategic significance of Arctic energy resources are the common key concern of Chinese academia, China's major energy enterprises, and China's influential mass media. Thus, we can argue that all of them are crucial functional actors in China in the securitizing move of Arctic energy affairs and have already made great efforts to promote this securitizing move discursively. Furthermore, it is worth noting that all the aforementioned major energy enterprises and mass media are state-affiliated, and their opinions are generally consistent with that of the state.

According to China's "Holistic View of National Security" ("总体国家安全观") and China's "National Security Law", resource security, including energy security, is an integral part of China's national security (China's Public Communication Office of National Security, 2021). China, the state, plays a role as the securitizing actor in securitizing Arctic energy resources in China, although the term "energy security" or more broadly- "resource security" has never been directly mentioned in the state's official discourses. In China's most important Arctic White Paper, the state pointed out the potential vital influence of Arctic energy resources on China's domestic energy policy and economic vitality: as "a major … energy consumer in the world", the "exploration and development of the resources in the Arctic may have a huge impact on the energy strategy and economic development of China" (State Council Information Office of the PRC, 2018). The State-owned Assets Supervision and Administration Commission of the State Council also pinpointed that China's involvement in Arctic LNG projects can offer more cost-effective gas and diversify the state's energy supply (State-owned Assets Supervision and Administration Commission of the State Council, 2019). It is worth noting that these arguments indicate the strategic importance of Arctic energy resources for the state, despite the exact use of 'security' in official discourses is missing.

Besides its relatively subtle official discourses, the state has been actively involved in exploring and developing Arctic energy resources in practice via international cooperation, which is a key pillar of China's PSR. The state has made noteworthy financial investments via state-owned energy enterprises and state-owned investment funds in large-scale Russian LNG projects – Yamal LNG and the Arctic LNG 2, occupying 29.9 percent and 20 percent of the share in these two LNG projects, respectively. Also, the state has signed huge purchase agreements with these two LNG projects, and CNPC made full value chain participation in the Yamal LNG project, not limited to investments and purchases (Liu, 2017). Although the state's official discourses are somewhat vague when it comes to energy security, the state has taken concrete actions, such as the above-mentioned noteworthy financial investments in Russian LNG projects, to obtain increasing energy supply from the Arctic and diversify its energy supply. This matches the core of the energy security concern highlighted by the functional actors.

However, according to the Copenhagen School of securitization theory, a securitizing move turns into a successful securitization only when in practice, the state as the securitizing actor manages to apply exceptional measures beyond normal politics. It is clear that none of the above-mentioned actions can be categorized as exceptional measures. In this sense, we argue that the state plays a role as a securitizing actor and is trying to construct China's energy supply as the referent object with functional actors together to securitize Arctic energy affairs, although it does not strictly follow the grammar of the Copenhagen School's securitization theory. Also, it seems the state's relatively 'vague' speech acts can still be effective to initiate and promote actions in China's political and social contexts. Such a 'vagueness' in the official discourses related to Arctic energy affairs may reflect China's general circumspect position when participating in Arctic affairs (Wang, Y., 2020). Most of the main players in the Arctic are Western states and the members of the North Atlantic Treaty Organization (NATO), which creates a sensitive political environment for China's participation, especially being a non-Arctic state and a rising non-Western great power.

The above-mentioned arguments on China's circumspect position may be challenged by so-called China's "wolf warrior" diplomacy, particularly increased and sharpened during *Xi's* presidency (Dai & LuQiu, 2021; Dettmer, 2020). However, it should be noted that China's "wolf warrior" diplomacy is largely limited to "defending China's core interests" (Dai & LuQiu, 2021, p. 2), such as "terrorism and human rights" and "Taiwan/One China" issues (Dai & LuQiu, 2021, pp. 20-22). Arctic-related affairs are not a part of China's core interests yet. Additionally, although China's diplomatic language has been getting more assertive and hostile to some extent, Chinese diplomacy has been historically shaped by traditional Chinese cultural traditions, such as Confucianism highlighting the importance of circumspection in interactions. The traditional Chinese cultural traditions still play a role in China's official discourses in international affairs, including Arctic affairs (Carnegie Endowment for International Peace, 2015).

In the speech acts, the referent object (China's energy supply) has been clearly constructed under existential threats, but the securitizing actor (the state) and the functional actors (Chinese academia, China's major energy enterprises, and China's mass media) do not present that it is Arctic energy resources that make China's energy supply an alarming issue or under threat. Instead, their speech acts created a clear image that Arctic energy affairs are of security and other strategic significance for China, which reveals a somewhat counterfactual logic: if China does not react to the emerging Arctic energy affairs timely and seriously, China's energy supply and the diversification of its supply cannot be improved, and China's domestic energy crisis would worsen. Interestingly, such logic seems to be effective enough in China as a starting point to convince the audience – the power elite, since China has been actively involved in exploring Arctic energy resources and promoting its PSR proposal.

In other words, China's energy security can benefit from Arctic energy resources. This seems to suggest China's securitization process of Arctic energy resources in the traditional energy sector is triggered by both threats (domestic energy crisis/ the lack of energy supply) and benefits (enormous energy supply and diversification of energy supply), and benefits play a more important role in this securitizing move. We may argue that Arctic energy affairs have become a priority of the state's political agenda, and the state has been taking actions to actively participate in Arctic energy security affairs to secure its domestic energy supply, such as strategically proposing the PSR and being largely involved in Arctic LNG projects. Although these actions may not be regarded as exceptional measures based on the Copenhagen School's securitization theory, we can still argue that there is an ongoing securitizing move of Arctic energy resources in the traditional energy security sector in China triggered by both threats and benefits, led by the state as the securitizing actor and facilitated by various functional actors in China. It might also be worth noting that the current dynamics of China's securitizing move of Arctic energy resources in the traditional sense may be challenged by the new EU Arctic policy: the EU seeks a ban on all new fossil fuel projects in the Arctic (European Commission, 2021). In reality, China's access to Arctic energy resources mostly depends on Russia, which strongly criticizes the EU's call. Russian Deputy Prime Minister *Alexander Novak* pinpointed that the EU "is not motivated by anything, except political reasons" to propose this energy ban (TASS Russian News Agency, 2021), and Russia will keep exploring and developing Arctic energy resources (interview 3, 2021 in Reykjavik, Iceland). Still, it is doubtful that China will entirely ignore the call to ban new energy exploitation in the Arctic made by the leading world "normative power" (Manners, 2015) with three member states (Finland, Sweden, and Denmark) in the Arctic.

Arctic energy resources and China's non-traditional energy security
On the basis of ensuring a sufficient and stable energy supply, China's energy security also highlights the sustainability of energy and environmentally friendly energy usage (China's Public Communication Office of National Security, 2021). This section explores how China securitizes Arctic energy affairs in terms of non-traditional energy security. It argues that the state, as the securitizing actor, and China's influential mass media and China's major energy enterprises, as the functional actors, are making a securitizing move of Arctic energy affairs in the non-traditional energy security sector and constructing the sustainability of China's national energy system as the referent object.

At the Climate Ambition Summit 2020, President *Xi Jinping* announced that China "aims to have CO_2 emissions peak before 2030 and achieve carbon neutrality before 2060" (Xinhua News Agency, 2020). The '2030 carbon peak and 2060 carbon neutrality' goal is clearly stated as the major national strategy and becomes a key part of China's overall economic and social development strategy in the newly-published White Paper on "China's Policies and Actions for Addressing Climate Change" (State Council Information Office of the PRC, 2021). Achieving this ambitious goal means a thorough energy transition to a clean and sustainable energy system in China. In the Arctic context, China has been closely involved in investing in Arctic LNG projects and purchasing LNG from the Arctic region. LNG is commonly considered as "a cleaner fossil alternative" (Gasum, 2020) and "a reliable support and back-up for renewable energy" (The Center for Liquefied Natural Gas (CLNG), no year). Compared to other fossil fuels, such as coal and petroleum, LNG can greatly reduce carbon emissions (Elengy, no year), although inevitably, an environmental footprint still exists (CLNG, no year). There is debate regarding if LNG is truly clean and can contribute to carbon neutrality (Horne & MacNab, 2014; Swanson et al., 2020), but LNG is still generally considered "the cleanest fossil fuel" (Elengy, no year) and the best bridge to renewable energy and carbon neutrality (Kovachich, 2021). In China's context, LNG has been widely described as clean energy, although some Chinese experts argue that LNG can only be called "clean fuel" rather than "clean energy" (for example, Pang, 2014). Since this section aims to showcase how China securitizes Arctic energy affairs in the non-traditional energy security sector, the following arguments will follow the common 'clean energy' description of LNG in China's context, which does not mean we endorse this expression.

There are three main functional actors facilitating the traditional energy securitizing move: Chinese academia, China's influential mass media, and China's major energy enterprises. However, the dynamics is not the same when China securitizes Arctic energy affairs in the non-traditional energy security sector. When Chinese academia actively stressed the traditional security significance of Arctic energy resources, some Chinese scholars also mentioned that Arctic LNG could effectively support the clean energy supply, but they merely mentioned this point rather briefly (He & Yu, 2020; Li, 2016;

Sun & Wu, 2016). In other words, the traditional strategic understanding of energy security is predominant in Chinese academia. Compared to Chinese academia, China's influential mass media, such as *People's Daily*, *Xinhua News Agency*, *Guangming Daily*, and *Beijing Business Today* (北京商报), paid more attention to the significance of Arctic LNG on adding domestic clean energy supply and facilitating domestic energy transition (Beijing Business Today, 2021; Lin, 2016; Ran, 2018; Yang, 2018; Zhang X. D., 2017; Zhang, Y., 2017). China's major energy enterprises, mainly CNPC with the full value chain participation in Arctic LNG projects, also articulated a similar opinion: Arctic LNG can provide China with clean energy supply and promote China's green energy transition (see CNPC, 2017; CNPC, 2018; Ding, Wu, & Xu, 2019; Meng & Liu, 2017). Moreover, in the discourses, China's influential mass media and major energy enterprises recognized the importance of Arctic clean energy resources to China's national energy system in which energy sustainability and the ongoing energy transition are challenged. However, no exact 'security' expressions can be noted in the discourses when highlighting Arctic clean energy resources' significance, although clean and low-carbon energy transition has been a great priority on China's political agenda.

The state, the securitizing actor in the traditional energy securitizing move, also stressed the importance of the Arctic clean energy resources and proposed action plans in a less straightforward way. For example, China's Arctic White Paper attended to the abundance of clean energy resources in the Arctic and highlighted that China "will work with the Arctic States to strengthen clean energy cooperation, […] explore the supply of clean energy and energy substitution and pursue low-carbon development" (State Council Information Office of the PRC, 2018). What is more, as *Nyman* and *Zeng* (2016) pointed out, there has been a new focus in China's Five-Year Plans (FYP) on optimizing energy production and consumption structure, in particular greatly developing clean energy and renewable energy, since the 11th FYP (2006-2010) (p. 308). In the most recent 14th FYP

(2021-2025), clean energy and low-carbon development were mentioned frequently. Developing the PSR and enhancing cooperation with the Arctic states is also a part of the 14th FYP (Xinhua News Agency, 2021). Since energy cooperation is the most important pillar of the PSR so far, these statements in the 14th FYP indicate that China will keep closely participating in the exploration and development of Arctic energy resources, especially clean energy resources, at least in the following five years.

Similar to the discourses of China's influential mass media and major energy enterprises, there are also no direct security expressions in that of the state. However, it is worth noting that their statements related to Arctic clean energy resources are all consistent with the non-traditional energy security understandings in general, especially with the understanding of energy security in China's "Holistic View of National Security" - valuing the sustainability of energy and the environmentally friendly use of energy (China's Public Communication Office of National Security, 2021). In this securitizing move of Arctic energy affairs in the non-traditional energy security sector, the sustainability of China's national energy system is constructed as the referent object under threat. Generally speaking, despite the declining ratio, coal still plays a dominant role in China's energy system, which is difficult to change thoroughly in the short-term (Pang, 2021). The heavy dependence on coal puts the sustainability of China's energy system under threat. However, more importantly, the Arctic energy resources can offer a stable supply of clean energy to China, which can promote China's domestic clean energy transition and improve the struggling sustainability issue of China's energy system. Thus, we argue that both threats and benefits triggered China's securitizing move of Arctic energy affairs in the non-traditional energy security sector, but much more attention was paid to benefits in the discourses of the securitizing actor and the functional actors. Similar to the securitizing move in the traditional energy security sector, a counterfactual logic can also be noted here. If China does not react to the affairs related to Arctic clean energy resources timely and seriously, the sustainability of China's national energy system will stay under threat, and the carbon neutrality goal will turn out to be more difficult to achieve. Last but not least, although we argue China's securitizing moves of Arctic energy affairs are ongoing in both the traditional energy security sector and the non-traditional energy security sector, there is a long path ahead for such securitizing moves to be successful securitization cases (if they even could be successfully securitized). The main reason is that there is no space for China as a non-Arctic state to exert measures beyond normal politics towards Arctic energy affairs.

Conclusion

Drawing on Copenhagen School's securitization theory, this chapter delves into China's securitization of Arctic climate change and Arctic energy affairs. By analyzing the speech acts of the securitizing actor (the state) and functional actors (Chinese academia, mass media, energy enterprises), we argue that China's securitization of Arctic climate change and energy affairs from both traditional and non-traditional security perspectives is still shown as ongoing securitizing moves, which are far from successful securitization cases with exceptional measures beyond normal politics. This chapter also looks into the interactions among the securitizing actor and functional actors in each securitizing move, further showcasing nuances and dynamics of securitization practices of the Arctic in the Chinese context.

With regards to Arctic climate change, the securitizing actor (the state) and the functional actors (Chinese academia, Chinese influential mass media) co-construct China (the state itself and people's livelihood) as the referent object under existential threats of Arctic climate change. This enables China to establish connections with the Arctic in an array of areas, such as scientific research, environment, economy, energy, and so forth, and therefore, establishing its identity as a key "stakeholder" and a "near-Arctic state" and justifying its increasing involvement in Arctic affairs. Targeting international audiences, the state also constructs the Arctic region as the other referent object threatened by the accelerated climate change, and, meanwhile, portrays itself as a responsible contributor to the vulnerable Arctic under threats. In this way, the state could mitigate international suspicions and doubts towards its Arctic participation as a non-Arctic actor and a rising non-Western power.

In the realm of Arctic energy affairs, the securitizing actor (the state) and the functional actors (Chinese academia, Chinese influential mass media, and Chinese major energy enterprises) construct China's energy supply as the referent objects together in the traditional energy security sector. In the non-traditional energy security sector, the same securitizing actor and functional actors, except for Chinese academia, co-construct the sustainability of China's national energy system as the referent object. In Chinese academia, the traditional strategic logic still plays a dominant role in understanding energy security. It should be noted that the logic behind the securitizing moves of Arctic energy affairs in China is different from that of Copenhagen School's securitization theory. We argue that both threats and potential benefits trigger such securitizing moves, and it seems benefits play a more important role. This indicates a counterfactual logic: China's energy supply and the sustainability of its national energy system are under threat but not because of Arctic energy affairs. Instead, the situations of the referent objects would worsen if China does not act on Arctic energy affairs timely and seriously.

Moreover, although securitizing moves of Arctic climate change and Arctic energy affairs are ongoing in China, they are not close to being successfully securitized. No exceptional measures beyond normal politics can be found, although some actions have been undertaken in China in response to its securitizing discourses, such as increasingly active involvement in Arctic LNG projects. More importantly, China, as a non-Arctic state and a rising non-Western power, does not have space to exert any measures beyond general rules or normal politics in the Arctic. Also, since the Arctic is not a part of China's core interests (China's discourse style towards Arctic affairs is far from its more assertive and hostile discourses when defending its core national interests), we could not see a possibility that

China may adopt exceptional measures in an indirect or a hidden way to securitize Arctic affairs, at least in the foreseeable future.

Shedding light on an array of research that applies the Copenhagen School's securitization theory on analyzing the securitization of the Arctic, this study highlights securitization dynamics in the non-Western Chinese context. It is different from most examinations of the Copenhagen School of securitization practices in Western democratic political systems where the general public is the typical audience. In this research, the main audience is the Chinese power elite, even though the Chinese mass media and the state also attempt to convince the general public and the international audience, respectively. Another key finding is the counterfactual logic in China's securitizing moves of Arctic energy affairs. However, it requires more case studies and in-depth analysis to find out whether this is a rare case or a more general tendency in China's securitizing moves of international affairs.

Notes

1. The Polar regions include the Antarctic and the Arctic, but the Arctic has more effects on China's holistic national security. This is because the Arctic has more geographical proximity for China (the main basis of China's 'near-Arctic state' identity construction) and is experiencing more considerably intensified game-playing among international participants, compared to the relatively stable Antarctic regulated by the Antarctic Treaty System.

2. Generally speaking, the term "near-Arctic state" highlights the wide connections between China and the Arctic, in terms of geographical proximity, economic connections, climate change, geopolitical impact, and so forth (for example, Liu, 2012; Lu, 2010; Lu & Zhang, 2016; Xinhua News Agency, 2013), to legitimize China's increasing interests and participation in the Arctic. The term was initially proposed by *Zhang Xia* in 2010, the then director of Polar Strategy Research Office of PRIC to address the geographical proximity between China and the Arctic, and to separate China from the wider

non-Arctic states (Lu, 2010, p. 339). It first appeared on an international occasion in November 2012, when the former Chinese Ambassador to Sweden, *Lan Lijun,* delivered a speech at an observer meeting held in Sweden (Xu & Wang, 2021, p. 145). This term did not get much attention in the early 2010s (Rainwater, 2013; SIPRI, 2012). However, it has gotten rapidly increasing international attention since China published its first-ever Arctic White Paper in 2018, in which China officially adopted this identity, and since Pompeo denied the third category between 'Arctic States' and 'Non-Arctic State' in his speech on the Arctic Council Ministerial in 2019 (Radio Canada International, 2019).

3. According to the latest research of the National Aeronautics and Space Administration (NASA), the United Kingdom's Met Office, and the Finnish Meteorological Institute, the Arctic is warming four times faster than the rest of the world in the past 30 years (Voosen, 2021).

Acknowledgements

The authors would like to thank Prof. Stefan Kirchner, Prof. Klaus Dodds, Prof. Juha Vuori, and Dr. Rachael Squire for their helpful comments and suggestions on the original manuscript. Any errors that remain are the authors' own.

Funding

Yue Wang's work on this chapter is funded by the Faculty of Management and Business, Tampere University, Finland. Liling Xu's work on this chapter is funded by the China Scholarship Council "International Regional Issues Research and Foreign Language High-level Talent Training Project", Project Number: [2019] 208 （国家留学基金委"国际区域问题研究及外语高层次人才培养项目"阶段成果, 项目号；留金欧［2019］208 号） and the "College Studentship" from the Department of Geography at Royal Holloway, University of London, the UK.

References

1. An, D. P., Wang, Q. R., Qin, Q, L., & Wu, M. (2018, December 11). 习总书记能源足迹| "冰上丝路"穿越北极—亚马尔液化天然气项目翻开中俄能源合作新篇章 [President Xi's Energy Footprint | The "Polar Silk Road" crossing the Arctic- Yamal LNG project opens a new chapter to enhance Sino-Russian energy cooperation]. *中国石油天然气集团有限公司 [China National Petroleum Corporation]*. http://www.cnpc.com.cn/cnpc/mtjj/201812/0fef16ef-baf04f4d920377d2dfbe4468.shtml.

2. Andersson, P. (2021). The Arctic as a "strategic" and "important" Chinese foreign policy interest: Exploring the role

of labels and hierarchies in China's Arctic discourses. *Journal of Current Chinese Affairs*, 106-136. https://doi.org/10.1177/18681026211018699.
3. Arctic Monitoring & Assessment Programme. (2021). *Arctic climate change update 2021: Key trends and impacts*. https://www.amap.no/documents/doc/arctic-climate-change-update-2021-key-trends-and-impacts.-summary-for-policy-makers/3508.
4. Arctic Council. (no year). Observers. *Arctic Council*. https://arcticcouncil.org/about/ observers/.
5. Arctic Council. (no year). About the Arctic Council. *Arctic Council*. https://arcticcouncil.org/ about/.
6. Åtland, K. (2008). Mikhail Gorbachev, the Murmansk Initiative, and the desecuritization of interstate relations in the Arctic. *Cooperation and Conflict*, *43*(3), 289-311. https://doi.org/10.1177/0010836708092838.
7. Beijing Business Today (2021, July 14). 2025年北京煤炭消费量将减至 100 万吨内 [Coal consumption in Beijing will be reduced to less than 1 million tons in 2025]. *北京商报 [Beijing Business Today]*.
8. Bo, Y. (2016). Securitization and Chinese Climate Change Policy. *Chinese Political Science Review*, *1*(1), 94-112. https://doi.org/10.1007/S41111-016-0003-5.
9. Brady, A. M. (2017). China as a polar great power. Cambridge University Press.
10. Brauch, G. H., & Scheffran, J. (2012). Introduction: Climate change, human security, and violent conflict in the anthropocene. In Scheffran, J., Brzoska, M., Brauch, G. H.,

Link, M. P, & Schilling, J. (Eds.), *Climate Change, Human Security and Violent Conflict* (pp. 3-40). Springer.
11. Buzan, B., Waever, O., & de Wilde, J. (1998). *Security: A new framework for analysis*. Lynne Rienner.
12. Buzan, B., & Hansen, L. (2009). The evolution of international security studies. Cambridge University Press.
13. Buzan, B., & Hansen, L. (2017). Defining - redefining security. In Denemark, R. A., & Marlin-Bennett, R. (Eds.), *The international studies encyclopedia*. Wiley-Blackwell. https://doi.org/10.1093/acref/9780191842665.001.0001.
14. Caballero-Anthony, M., & Putra, N. A. (2012). Introduction: Energy and non-traditional security (NTS) - Understanding security from below. In Caballero-Anthony, M., Chang, Y., & Putra, N. A. (Eds.), *Energy and non-Traditional security (NTS) in Asia* (pp. 1-11). Springer. https://link.springer.com/book/10.1007/978-3-642-29706-9.
15. Cambou, D., & Hossain, K. (2019). *Society, environment and human security in the Arctic barents region.* Routledge.
16. Carnegie Endowment for International Peace. (2015, December 15). How traditional culture shapes Chinese diplomacy. *Carnegie Endowment for International Peace.* https://carnegieendowment.org/2015/12/15/how-traditional-culture-shapes-chinese-diplomacy-event-5104.
17. Center for Liquefied Natural Gas. (no year). LNG and the environment. *The Center for Liquefied Natural Gas.* https://www.lngfacts.org/lng-and-the-environment/.
18. Chen, M. (2012). 中国能源安全新思考 [New thoughts on China's energy security]. *西亚非洲 [West Asia and Africa],* (6), 94-112.

19. China National Petroleum Corporation. (2017, December 13). 全球最大北极液化天然气项目首船发运 [The world's largest Arctic LNG project shipped for the first time]. *中国石油天然气集团有限公司 [China National Petroleum Corporation]*. http://www.cnpc.com.cn/cnpc/mtjj/201712/5478431742d5470c90b065abf42af5b6.shtml.

20. China National Petroleum Corporation. (2018, October 30). 中国天然气进口：改写格局的力量 [China's natural gas imports: the power to change its energy system]. *中国石油天然气集团有限公司 [China National Petroleum Corporation]*. http://news.cnpc.com.cn/system/2018/10/26/001708690.shtml.

21. China National Petroleum Corporation. (2020, December 2). 北极的油气资源 [Oil and gas resources in the Arctic]. *中国石油天然气集团有限公司 [China National Petroleum Corporation]*. http://www.cnpc.com.cn/syzs/ktkf/202012/82c04e1fed7e4c6e87f28a766b796931.shtml.

22. China News Service. (2018, January 27). 解读中国的北极政策白皮书:明确自身定位助推国际合作[Interpretation of China's White Paper on Arctic Policy: Clarify its own position and promote international cooperation]. *中新社 [China News Service]*. https://www.chinanews.com.cn/gn/2018/01-27/8434669.shtml.

23. China's Public Communication Office of National Security. (2021, April 14). 总体国家安全观的"16 种安全" ["16

types of security" of China's holistic view of national security]. 国安宣工作室 *[China's Public Communication Office of National Security].* http://www.stdaily.com/cehua/20210414/202104/14/content_1114342.shtml.

24. Chinese Antarctic Center of Surveying and Mapping, Wuhan University. (2017, October 11). 国家海洋局举行新闻发布会 我国北极考察正式进入常态化 [State Oceanic Administration held a press conference: China's Arctic expedition officially became normalization]. *Chinese Antarctic Center of Surveying and Mapping, Wuhan University.* http://pole.whu.edu.cn/cacsm/gb_news.php?modid=02001&id=131166.

25. Cornell, P. E. (2009). Energy and the three levels of national security: Differentiating energy concerns within a national security context. *Connections: The Quarterly Journal, 8*(4), 63-80. http://dx.doi.org/10.11610/Connections.08.4.04.

26. Dai, Y. (2021). "冰上丝绸之路"倡议下北极航道的中国话语权构建 [The construction of China's discursive right of Arctic shipping routes under the "Polar Silk Road" initiative]. *理论界 [Theory Horizon],* (8), 81-87.

27. Dai, Y. Y., & Luqiu, L. W. (2021). Wolf warriors and Xi Jinping's diplomacy: An empirical analysis of China's diplomatic language. Preprint on ResearchGate. https://www.researchgate.net/publication/350677590_China's_Wolf_Warrior_Diplomacy_and_Xi_Jinping's_Grand_Diplomatic_Strategy.

28. De Botselier, B., López Piqueres, S., & Schunz, S. (2018). Addressing the "Arctic Paradox": Environmental policy integration. *European Union's Emerging Arctic Policy*, 3, https://www.coleurope.eu/sites/default/files/research-paper-covers/cover_edp_2018_03_0.png.

29. Deng, B. X. (2020). 北极安全研究 [*Arctic security studies*]. 海洋出版社 [China Ocean Press].

30. Dettmer, J. (2020, May 6). China's 'Wolf Warrior' diplomacy prompts international backlash. *Voice of America (VOA)*. https://www.voanews.com/a/covid-19-pandemic_chinas-wolf-warrior-diplomacy-prompts-international-backlash/6188830.html.

31. Devyatkin, P. (2018). Russia's Arctic strategy: Energy extraction (Part III). *The Arctic Institute: Center for Circumpolar Security Studies*. https://www.thearcticinstitute.org/russias-arctic-strategy-energy-extraction-part-three/.

32. Ding, J. G., Wu, M., & Xu, T. (2019, July 22). 中俄油气合作进入新阶段 中国石油完成北极 LNG2 项目收购全部手续 [Sino-Russian oil and gas cooperation enters a new stage: CNPC completes all procedures for the acquisition of the Arctic LNG2 project]. *中国石油天然气集团有限公司 [China National Petroleum Corporation]*. http://www.cnpc.com.cn/cnpc/gjmyxgdt/201907/bec1b069d2a54e668308b998a4fadf0a.shtml.

33. Dodds, K., & Nuttall, M. (2015). *The scramble for the poles: The geopolitics of the Arctic and Antarctic.* Polity Press.

34. Doshi, R., Dale-Huang, A., & Zhang, G. (2021). *Northern expedition: China's Arctic activities and ambitions.* https://www.brookings.edu/research/northern-expedition-chinas-arctic-activities-and-ambitions/.
35. Elengy. (no year). LNG: An energy of the future. *Elengy.* https://www.elengy.com/en/local-residents/lng-an-energy-of-the future.html#:~:text=LNG%20is%20the%20cleanest%20fossil,and%20help%20combat%20global%20warming.
36. Ellinas, C. (2020, June 26). China and energy security. *Natural Gas News.* https://www.naturalgasworld.com/china-and-energy-security-ngw-magazine-79882.
37. Eroukhmanoff, C. (2018). Securitisation theory: An introduction. *E-International Relations.* https://www.e-ir.info/2018/01/14/securitisation-theory-an-introduction/.
38. European Commission (2021). Joint communication to the European Parliament, the Council, the European Economic and Social Committee and the Committee of the Regions: A stronger EU engagement for a peaceful, sustainable and prosperous Arctic. *European Commission.* https://ec.europa.eu/commission/presscorner/detail/en/ip_21_5214.
39. Feng, H. Y., He, K., & Yan, X. T. (2019). *Chinese scholars and foreign policy: Debating international relations.* Routledge.
40. Financial Times. (2007, August 19). Scramble for the Arctic. *Financial Times.* https://www.ft.com/content/65b9692c-4e6f-11dc-85e7-0000779fd2ac.

41. Freeman, D. (2010). The missing link: China, climate change and national security. *SSRN Electronic Journal.* https://doi.org/10.2139/SSRN.2695409.
42. Gasum. (2020). LNG – Clean energy for the Nordic countries. *Gasum.* https://www.gasum.com/en/insights/energy--industry/2020/liquefied-natural-gas---lng/.
43. Gautier, D. L., Bird, K.J., Charpentier, R. R., Grantz, A., Houseknecht, D., Klett, R. T., & Moore, E. T., & Pitman, K. J., Schenk, J. C., Schuenemeyer, H. J., Sørensen, K., Tennyson, E. M., Valin, C. Z. & Wandrey, C. (2009). Assessment of undiscovered oil and gas in the Arctic. *Science, 324*(5931), 1175-1179. https://doi.org/10.1126/science.1169467.
44. Gorbachev, M. (1987). *The Speech in Murmansk at the ceremonial meeting on the occasion of the presentation of the Order of Lenin and the Gold Star Medal to the city of Murmansk, October 1, 1987.* Novosti Press Agency.
45. Greaves, W., & Pomerants, D. (2017). 'Soft Securitization': Unconventional security issues and the Arctic Council. *Politik, 20*(3), 31-46. https://doi.org/10.7146/POLITIK.V20I3.97152.
46. Gricius, G. (2021). The Arctic's securitization. *Inkstick Media.* https://inkstickmedia.com/the-arctics-securitization.
47. Gross, M. (2020). Arctic meltdown. *Current Biology, 30*(23), 1391. https://doi.org/10.1016/J.CUB.2020.11.023.
48. Guan. K. J., Pei, G. J., Wan, Y., Qu, S., & Huang, Y. D. (2018, January 28). "冰上丝绸之路"吸引世界目光 ["Polar Silk Road" attracts the world's attention]. 人民日报 *[People's Daily].* http://world.people.com.cn/n1/2018/0128/c1002-29790791.html.

49. Haas, P. (1992). Introduction: Epistemic communities and international policy coordination. *International Organization, 46*(1), 1-35. doi:10.1017/S0020818300001442.
50. Hansen, L. (2000). The little mermaid's silent security dilemma and the absence of gender in the Copenhagen School. *Millennium: Journal of International Studies, 29*(2), 285-306. https://doi.org/10.1177/03058298000290020501.
51. He, Y. M., & Yu, T. (2020). "一带一路" 背景下中俄合作开发北极油气资源前景 [Prospects for Sino-Russian cooperation in developing Arctic oil and gas resources under the background of the "Belt and Road Initiative"]. 中国石油大学学报（社会科学版）*[Journal of China University of Petroleum (Edition of Social Sciences)], 36*(2), 14-19. https://doi.org/10.13216 /j.cnki.upcjess.2020.02.0002.
52. Heggelund, G., & Han, C. (2019). China's climate policy: Does an Arctic dimension exist? *Arctic Governance Volume III, 27*(3), 139-145. https://doi.org/10.5040/9781838600099.ch-013.
53. Heininen, L., Exner-Pirot, H., & Barnes, J. (Eds.) (2019). *Arctic Yearbook 2019 - Redefining Arctic Security*, Arctic Portal. https://issuu.com/arcticportal/docs/ay2019.
54. Hong, N. (2020). *China's role in the Arctic: Observing and being observed*. Routledge.
55. Horne, M., & MacNab, J. (2014). LNG and climate change: The global context. *Pacific Institute for Climate Solutions*. https://www.pembina.org/reports/lng-and-climate-change-the-global-context-pi-pics.pdf.

56. Hsiung, C. W. (2016). China and Arctic energy: Drivers and limitations. *The Polar Journal, 6*(2), 243-258. http://dx.doi.org/10.1080/2154896X.2016.1241486.
57. International Energy Agency. (no year). *Data browser - China.* https://www.iea.org/countries/china.
58. Jacobsen, M., & Herrmann, V. (2017). Introduction: Arctic international relations in a widened security perspective. *Politik*, *20*(3), 6-14. https://doi.org/10.7146/politik.v20i3.97174.
59. Jacobsen, M., & Strandsbjerg, J. (2017). Desecuritization as displacement of controversy: geopolitics, law and sovereign rights in the Arctic. *Politik*, *20*(3), 15-30. https://doi.org/10.7146/politik.v20i3.97151.
60. Jakobson, L. (2015). China's security and the Arctic. In Dittmer, L. & Yu, M. (Eds.), *Routledge Handbook of Chinese Security* (pp. 155-166). Routledge Handbooks Online. https://doi.org/10.4324/9781315712970.CH10.
61. Jia, L. X. (2017, July 13). 北极地区油气资源勘探开发现状 [Status Quo of exploration and development of oil and gas resources in the Arctic]. *中国矿业报 [China Mining News]*.
62. Jiang, N. (2018, February 16). 一封寄自北极圈的家书（寄给祖国的家书）[A letter from the Arctic Circle (A letter to the motherland)]. *人民日报 [People's Daily]*. http://world.people.com.cn/n1/2018/0216/c1002-29825136.html.
63. Käpylä, J., & Mikkola, H. (2013). Arctic conflict potential: Towards an extra-Arctic perspective. *The Finnish Institute*

of International Affairs (FIIA) briefing paper (138). https://www.fiia.fi/en/publication/arctic-conflict-potential?read.

64. Kiesow, L. (2004). China's quest for energy: Impact upon foreign and security policy. *Swedish Defence Research Agency: User report FOI- R- 1371 - SE.*

65. Kovachich, L. (2021, June 25). 中国按动天然气阀:蓝色燃料或成能源转型桥梁 [China presses the natural gas valve: Blue fuel may become a bridge for energy transition]. *Sputnik News.* https://sputniknews.cn/economics/20210625 1033959917/.

66. Lanteigne, M. (2015). The role of China in emerging Arctic security discourses. *Security and Peace, 33*(3), 150-155. https://www.jstor.org/stable/26389207?seq=1#metadata_info_tab_contents.

67. Lei, S., & Yin, J. Y. (2014). 北极油气开发现状与战略思考 [Arctic petroleum development: Status quo and China's oil companies' strategy]. *中国矿业 [China Mining Magazine], 23*(2), 16-23.

68. Li, B. (2001, February 1). "中国首次北极科学考察"通过验收 ["China's first Arctic scientific expedition" passed the acceptance test]. *光明日报 [Guangming Daily].* https://www.gmw.cn/01gmrb/2001-02/01/GB/02%5E18679%5E0%5EGMA2-007.htm.

69. Li, X. (2016). 中俄油气合作新发展的特征、动因及影响探析 [Analysis of characteristics, motivation and impact of the breakthrough of Sino-Russian oil and gas cooperation].

国际论坛 *[International Forum], 18*(1), 33-40. https://doi.org/10.13549/j.cnki.cn11-3959/d.2016.01.006.

70. Li, Y. (2018, October 14). 69天往返北极的"中国航迹" [69 days - "China's shipping track" to and from the Arctic]. *北京青年报 [Beijing Youth Daily].* http://epaper.ynet.com/html/2018-10/14/content_306423.htm?div=-1.

71. Lin, X. D. (2016, May 11). 中俄扩大清洁能源合作 —亚马尔项目有望每年向中国供应300万吨液化天然气 [China and Russia expand clean energy cooperation-Yamal project is expected to supply 3 million tons of liquefied natural gas to China each year]. *人民日报 [People's Daily].* http://world.people.com.cn/n1/2016/0511/c1002-28340117.html.

72. Liu, P., & Hu, M. X. (2016). 北极航道开通对我国能源供求形势的影响 [Impact of the opening of Arctic waterway on China's energy supply and demand situation]. *海洋开发与管理 [Ocean Development and Management],* (8), 80-83.

73. Liu, S. S. (2012). "近北极机制"的提出与中国参与北极 [The Proposal of the "Near Arctic Mechanism" and China's Participation in the Arctic]. *社会科学 [Social Science]*, (10), 26-34.

74. Liu, X. (2017, December 27). 来自"冰上丝路"的天然气 [The natural gas from the "Polar Silk Road"]. *环球杂志，新华社 [The Global Magazine, Xinhua News Agency].* http://www.xinhuanet.com/globe/2018-01/01/c_136857530.htm.

75. Lu, J. Y. (2010). *北极地缘政治与中国应对 [Geopolitics in the Arctic and China's Response]*. 时事出版社 [Current Affairs Press].
76. Lu, J. Y., & Zhang, X. (2016). *中国北极权益与政策研究 [China's Arctic Interests and Policy]*. 时事出版社[Current Affairs Press].
77. Luhn, A. (2020, October 16). Freezing cold war: Militaries move in as Arctic ice retreats. *The Guardian*. https://www.theguardian.com/environment/2020/oct/16/arctic-ice-retreats-climate-us-russian-canadian-chinese-military.
78. Luo, Y. J. (2018, December 26). 开拓北极航道 共建"冰上丝路" [Open up the Arctic waterway and jointly build the "Polar Silk Road"]. *光明日报 [Guangming Daily]*. https://epaper.gmw.cn/gmrb/html/2018-12/26/nw.D110000gmrb_20181226_3-12.htm.
79. Manners, I. (2015). The European Union in global politics: Normative power and longitudinal interpretation. In Lynggaard, K., Manners, I., & Löfgren, K. (Eds.), *Research methods in European Union studies* (pp.221-236). Palgrave Studies in European Union Politics. Palgrave Macmillan. https://doi.org/10.1057/9781137316967_14.
80. Meng, Q. L., & Liu, Y. (2017, July 7). 王宜林赴亚马尔液化天然气项目现场调研强调：全力配合第一条生产线按期投产 扩大合作共同开发北极油气资源 [Wang Yilin investigated the Yamal LNG project on-site investigation and emphasized to ensure the first production line to put into

production on schedule, expand cooperation and jointly develop Arctic oil and gas resources]. 中国石油天然气集团有限公司 *[China National Petroleum Corporation].* https://www.cnpc.com.cn/cnpc/jtxw/201707/2dd8838fb8d345ffbb359d3bfac5f3d5.shtml.

81. Miller, S. E. (2001). International security at twenty-five: From one world to another. *International Security, 26*(1), 5-39. https://www.jstor.org/stable/3092077.

82. Ministry of Foreign Affairs of the PRC (2015, October 17). Keynote speech by Vice Minister of Foreign Affairs *Zhang Ming* at the China's session of the third Arctic Circle Assembly. *Ministry of Foreign Affairs of the PRC.* https://www.fmprc.gov.cn/mfa_eng/wjdt_665385/zyjh_665391/201510/t20151017_678393.html

83. Ministry of Foreign Affairs of the PRC. (2017, June 14). 第二轮中日韩北极事务高级别对话联合声明 [Joint Statement on the second Trilateral High-Level Dialogue on the Arctic]. *Ministry of Foreign Affairs of the PRC.* https://www.fmprc.gov.cn/web/wjb_673085/zzjg_673183/tyfls_674667/xwlb_674669/201706/t20170614_7670739.shtml.

84. Ministry of Foreign Affairs of the PRC. (2019, May 8). Foreign Ministry Spokesperson Geng Shuang's Regular Press Conference on May 8, 2019. *Ministry of Foreign Affairs of the PRC.* https://www.fmprc.gov.cn/fyrbt_673021/jzhsl_673025/201905/t20190508_5417491.shtml.

85. Mulligan, S. (2010). Energy, environment, and security: Critical links in a post-peak world. *Global Environmental Politics, 10*(4), 79-100. https://muse.jhu.edu/article/404384.

86. Nyman, J., & Zeng, J. H. (2016). Securitization in Chinese climate and energy politics. *Wiley Interdisciplinary Reviews: Climate Change, 7*(2), 301-313. https://doi.org/10.1002/WCC.387.

87. Olesen, M. R. (2014). Cooperation or conflict in the Arctic: A literature review. *Danish Institute of International Studies (DIIS) Working Paper 08.* https://pure.diis.dk/ws/files/70921/wp2014_08_Runge_Olesen_for_web.pdf.

88. Pan, M. (2014). 机遇与风险：北极环境变化对中国能源安全的影响及对策分析 [Opportunities and Risks: The impact of the Arctic environmental changes on China's energy security]. *中国软科学 [China Soft Science],* (9)*,* 12-21.

89. Pang, M. L. (2014, July 25). LNG 没你想象中那么美好 [LNG is not as good as you think]. *新浪财经 [Sina Finance].* http://finance.sina.com.cn/energy/spicycommentary/20140725/152719820946.shtml.

90. Pang, W. J. (2021, September 5). 经济观察：走向碳中和，中国火电如何转型？[Economic Observation: How will China's thermal power transit towards carbon neutrality?]. *中国新闻网 [China News Service].* https://www.chinanews.com.cn/cj/2021/09-05/9558861.shtml.

91. Radin, A., Scobell, A., Treyger, E., Williams, J. D., Ma, L., Shatz, H. J., Zeigler, S. M., Han, E., & Reach, C. (2021). China-Russia cooperation: Determining factors, future

trajectories, implications for the United States. *RAND Corporation*. https://www.rand.org/pubs/research_reports/RR3067.html.

92. Radio Canada International. (2019, May 6). U.S. stuns audience by tongue-lashing China, Russia on eve of Arctic Council ministerial. *The Barents Observer*. https://thebarentsobserver.com/en/arctic/2019/05/us-stuns-audience-tongue-lashing-china-russia-eve-arctic-council-ministerial.

93. Rainwater, S. (2013). Race to the North: China's Arctic strategy and its implications. *Naval War College Review*, *66*(2), 1-21. https://digital-commons.usnwc.edu/nwc-review/vol66/iss2/7.

94. Ran, Y. P. (2018, July 20). 中俄特大型能源合作项目首船亚马尔液化天然气运抵中国 [The first ship of Yamal LNG - the Sino-Russian mega-energy cooperation project- arrives in China]. 人民日报 *[People's Daily]*. http://energy.people.com.cn/n1/2018/0720/c71661-30161192.html.

95. Ren, J. M. (1999, August 20). 北极科考进入攻坚阶段[The Arctic expedition enters a critical stage]. 人民日报 *[People's Daily]*. http://www.people.com.cn/rmrb/199908/20/newfiles/wzb_19990820001046_5.html.

96. Rosamond, A. B. (2011). Perspectives on security in the Arctic area. *Danish Institute of International Studies (DIIS) Report,* (9). https://pure.diis.dk/ws/files/61204/RP2011_09_Arctic_security_web.pdf.

97. Sahu, A. K. (2021). From the climate change threat to the securitisation of development: An analysis of China. *China*

Report, 57(2), 192-209. https://doi.org/10.1177/00094455211004259.

98. Sandkelf, K. (2004). Energy in China: Coping with increasing demand. *Swedish Defence Research Agency: User report FOI- R- 1435 - SE.* https://inis.iaea.org/collection/NCLCollectionStore/_Public/36/045/36045273.pdf?r=1&r=1#:~:text=China%20is%20projected%20to%20increase,develop%20the%20current%20energy%20resources.

99. Saxena, A. (2020, October 22). The return of great power competition to the Arctic. *The Arctic Institute: Center for Circumpolar Security Studies.* https://www.thearcticinstitute.org/return-great-power-competition-arctic/.

100. School of International Studies, Peking University. (2012, November 17). "气候变化与国家安全战略的关键技术研究"课题启动会议在北大举行" ["Research on key technologies of climate change and national security strategy" project initiating meeting was held in Peking University]. *北京大学国际关系学院 [School of International Studies, Peking University].* https://www.sis.pku.edu.cn/news64/1302235.htm.

101. School of International Studies, Peking University (2016, June 22). "十二五"国家科技支撑计划课题"气候变化与国家安全战略的关键技术研究"顺利结项 [The "Twelfth Five-Year" national science and technology support program project "Key Technology Research on Climate Change and National Security Strategy" has been

successfully completed]. *北京大学国际关系学院 [School of International Studies, Peking University].* https://www.sis.pku.edu.cn/news64/1301875.htm.

102. Shanghai Institute for International Studies (2021, October 20). 我院联合举办北极圈论坛"冰上丝绸之路"主题分会 [Our institute jointly organized the "Polar Silk Road" session at the Arctic Circle Assembly]. *上海国际问题研究院 [Shanghai Institute for International Studies].* http://www.siis.org.cn/Content/Info/4UF306W5UPJJ.

103. SIPRI. (2012, May 10). China defines itself as a 'Near-arctic State', says SIPRI. *SIPRI.* https://www.sipri.org/media/press-release/2012/china-defines-itself-near-arctic-state-says-sipri.

104. Sørensen, C. T. N., & Klimenko, E. (2017). Emerging Chinese-Russian cooperation in the Arctic: Possibilities and constraints. *Stockholm International Peace Research Institute (SIPRI) policy paper*, (46). https://www.sipri.org/sites/default/files/2017-06/emerging-chinese-russian-cooperation-arctic.pdf.

105. Spivak, V. (2021, October 15). What does China's energy crisis mean for Russia? *The Moscow Times.* https://www.themoscowtimes.com/2021/10/15/what-does-chinas-energy-crisis-mean-for-russia-a75307.

106. State Council Information Office of the People's Republic of PRC. (2018). China's Arctic Policy. *State Council Information Office of the People's Republic of PRC.* http://english.www.gov.cn/archive/white_paper/2018/01/26/content_281476026660336.htm

107. State Council Information Office of the Peoples PRC. (2021, October). 中国应对气候变化的政策与行动 [China's Policies and Actions for Addressing Climate Change]. *新华社 [Xinhua News Agency]*. http://www.news.cn/2021-10/27/c_1128001009.htm.

108. State-Owned Assets Supervision and Administration Commission of the State Council. (2019, January 7). 他们来自北极！中国石油亚马尔团队的故事 [They are from the Arctic! The story of the CNPC Yamal team]. *国务院国有资产监督管理委员会 [The State-Owned Assets Supervision and Administration Commission of the State Council]*. http://www.sasac.gov.cn/n2588025/n2588119/c10197933/content.html.

109. Sun, K., & Ma, Y. H. (2018). "冰上丝绸之路"背景下的中俄北极能源合作—以亚马尔 LNG 项目为例 [China-Russia Arctic energy cooperation in the context of the "Polar Silk Road" – A case study of Yamal LNG project]. *中国海洋大学学报社会科学版 [Journal of Ocean University of China (Edition of Social Sciences)]*, *6*(1), 1-6. https://doi.org/ 10.16497/j.cnki.1672-335x.2018.06.001.

110. Sun, K., & Wu, H. (2016). 北极安全新态势与中国北极安全利益维护 [The new situation of Arctic security and the safeguarding of China's Arctic security interests]. *南京政治学院学报 [Journal of PLA Nanjing Institute of Politics]*, *32*(5), 71-77. https://doi.org/10.13231/j.cnki.jnip.2016.05.012.

111. Swanson, C., Levin, A., Stevenson, A., Mall, A., & Spencer, T. (2020). Sailing to nowhere: Liquefied natural gas is not an effective climate strategy. *The Natural Resources Defense Council*. https://www.nrdc.org/resources/sailing-nowhere-liquefied-natural-gas-not-effective-climate-strategy.

112. TASS Russian News Agency. (2021, October 15). Press review: China beefs up its nukes and EU pressing for bigger role in Arctic. *TASS Russian News Agency*. https://tass.com/pressreview/1349947.

113. The Third National Assessment Report on Climate Change Committee. (2015). 第三次气候变化国家评估报告 *[The third national assessment report on climate change]*. 科学出版社 [Science Press].

114. TotalEnergies. (no year). Yamal LNG: The gas that came in from the cold. *TotalEnergies*. https://totalenergies.com/energy-expertise/projects/oil-gas/lng/yamal-lng-cold-environment-gas#:~:text=A%20world%20leader%20in%20liquefied,located%20in%20Russia's%20Far%20North.

115. Trombetta, M. J. (2019). Securitization of climate change in China: Implications for global climate governance. *China Quarterly of International Strategic Studies*, 5(1), 97-116. https://doi.org/10.1142/S2377740019500076.

116. United States Geological Survey. (2008, December 31). *Assessment of undiscovered oil and gas in the arctic*. https://www.usgs.gov/publications/assessment-undiscovered-oil-and-gas-arctic.

117. United States International Trade Administration. (2021, February 4). *China country commercial guide: Energy*. https://www.trade.gov/country-commercial-guides/china-energy.
118. Voosen, P. (2021, December 14). The Arctic is warming four times faster than the rest of the world. *Science*, https://www.science.org/content/article/arctic-warming-four-times-faster-rest-world.
119. Vuori, J. A. (2008). Illocutionary logic and strands of securitization: Applying the theory of securitization to the study of non-democratic political orders. *European Journal of International Relations, 14*(1), 65-99. https://doi.org/10.1177/1354066107087767.
120. Vuori, J. A. (2011). *How to do security with words: A grammar of securitisation in the People's Republic of China* [Doctoral dissertation, University of Turku]. UTUPub (Institutional Repository). https://www.utupub.fi/bitstream/handle/10024/70743/AnnalesB336Vuori.pdf?sequence=1&isAllowed=y.
121. Vuori, J. A. (2016). Constructivism and securitization studies. In Cavelty, M. D., & Balzacq, T. (Eds.), *The routledge handbook of security studies* (2nd Edition) (pp. 64-74), Routledge.
122. Waever, O. (1995). Securitization and desecuritization. In Lipschutz, R. D. (Ed.), *On Security* (pp. 46–86). Columbia University Press. http://www.ciaonet.org/book/lipschutz/lipschutz13.html.
123. Waever, O. (2003). Securitisation: Taking stock of a research programme in Security Studies. Unpublished draft.

124. Waver, O. (2015). The theory act: Responsibility and exactitude as seen from securitization. *International Relations, 29*(1), 121-127. https://doi.org/10.1177/0047117814526606d.

125. Wang, C. X. (2013). 北极地区安全维度变化与北极地区议题安全化[Changes in the security dimension of the Arctic and the securitization of Arctic issues]. *国际安全研究[International Security Research], 31*(3), 101-115.

126. Wang, D. R. (2020). 北极的油气资源 [Oil and gas resources in the Arctic]. *石油知识 [Petroleum Knowledge],* (1), 8-9.

127. Wang, L. B., & Zhang, J. S. (2021, September 29). 中国第12次北极科学考察圆满完成[China's 12th Arctic scientific expedition was successfully completed]. *新华网 [Xinhua News]*. https://cn.chinadaily.com.cn/a/202109/29/WS6153a94ea3107be4979f0600.html.

128. Wang, M. L. (2020, September 25). 全球变暖 北极海冰或将消失[Global warming: Arctic sea ice may disappear]. *中国气象报 [China Meteorological News]*.

129. Wang, Y. (2020). A comparative study of the official use of Arctic environmental discourses of China and the EU. *The Arctic Institute: Center for Circumpolar Security Studies*. https://www.thearcticinstitute.org/comparative-study-official-use-arctic-environmental-discourses-china-eu/.

130. Wang, Y. C. (2021, October 28). 确保能源安全关键在保供 [The key to guarantee energy security is to guarantee energy supply]. *经济日报 [Economic Daily].*
131. Wilkinson, C. (2007). The Copenhagen school on tour in Kyrgyzstan: Is securitization theory useable outside Europe? *Security Dialogue, 38*(1), 5-25. https://doi.org/10.1177/0967010607075964.
132. Wishnick, E. (2019). Russia and the Arctic in China's quest for great-power status. In Tellis, J. A., Szalwinski, A. & Wills, M. (Eds.), *Strategic Asia 2019: China's Expanding Strategic Ambitions*. The National Bureau of Asian Research. https://www.nbr.org/publication/russia-and-the-arctic-in-chinas-quest-for-great-power-status/.
133. Wu, Y., & Qu, S. (2017, August 4). 中俄能源合作驶入快车道 [Sino-Russian energy cooperation enters the fast lane]. *人民日报 [People's Daily].* http://www.scio.gov.cn/31773/35507/35510/35524/Document/1560354/1560354.htm.
134. Xia, L. P. (2011). 北极环境变化对全球安全和中国国家安全的影响 [The impact of Arctic environmental changes on global security and China's national security]. *世界经济与政治 [World Economy and Politics]*, (1), 122-133.
135. Xiang, J. (2003, July 16). 聚焦北极科考[Focus on Arctic scientific research]. *人民网 [People's Website].* http://www.cctv.com/geography/20030716/100763.shtml.

136. Xiao, Y. (2016). 中俄共建 "北极能源走廊": 战略支点与推进理路 [the Sino-Russian co-construction of the Arctic energy corridor: Strategic fulcrum and promotion pathway]. 东北亚论坛 [*Northeast Asia Forum*], *127*(5), 109-117. https://10.13654/j.cnki.naf.2016.05.010.

137. Xinhua News Agency. (2013, March 23). 专访：中国愿为北极地区可持续发展作出贡献[Exclusive interview: China is willing to contribute to the independent development of the Arctic]. *新华社 [Xinhua News Agency]*. http://www.gov.cn/jrzg/2013-03/23/content_2360686.htm.

138. Xinhua News Agency. (2015, July 1). 中华人民共和国国家安全法（主席令第二十九号）[National security law of the People's Republic of China (President Order No. 29)]. *新华社 [Xinhua News Agency]*. http://www.gov.cn/zhengce/2015-07/01/content_2893902.htm.

139. Xinhua News Agency. (2020, December 12). 习近平在气候雄心峰会上的讲话（全文）[Full Text: Remarks by Chinese President Xi Jinping at Climate Ambition Summit]. *新华社 [Xinhua News Agency]*. http://www.xinhuanet.com/politics/leaders/2020-12/12/c_1126853600.htm.

140. Xinhua News Agency (2021, March 13). 中华人民共和国国民经济和社会发展第十四个五年规划和2035年远景目标纲要 [Outline of the People's Republic of China 14th Five-Year Plan for national economic and social development and long-range objectives for 2035]. *新华社*

[Xinhua News Agency]. http://www.gov.cn/xinwen/202103/13/content_5592681.htm.

141. Xu, Q. C., & Wang, H. M. (2021). 21世纪以来中国的北极研究:进展与问题—徐庆超助理研究员访谈 [Arctic research in China since the 21st century: Progress and questions]. 国际政治研究 [The Journal of International Studies], 42(4), 138-160.

142. Xu, Y. H. (2018, November 4). 港媒：中国将目光投向北极航线 "冰上丝路" 正在成形 [Hong Kong media: China sets its sights on the Arctic shipping routes and the "Polar Silk Road" is forming]. 参考消息 [Reference News]. http://www.cankaoxiaoxi.com/china/20181104/2347988_4.shtml.

143. Yang, Y. (2018, July 19). 北极天然气来了：中国首船亚马尔 LNG 经北极航道运抵江苏 [Arctic natural gas is here: China's first Yamal LNG vessel arrives in Jiangsu via the Arctic shipping route]. 澎湃新闻 [The Paper]. https://www.thepaper.cn/newsDetail_forward_2275369.

144. Yang, Z. J., Cui, J., Han, S. Y., Guo, P. Q., & Fan. H. Y. (2013). 北极生态安全对中国国家安全的影响及应对策略 [The Arctic ecological security impact on national security of China and strategy]. 海洋环境科学 [Marine Environmental Science], 32(4), 629-635.

145. Yang, Z. J., Sun, X. M., & Xin, M. J. (2015). 北极能源安全问题研究综述 [A literature review on Arctic energy security]. 中国海洋大学学报社会科学版 [Journal of

Ocean University of China (Edition of Social Sciences)], (5), 25-33. https://doi.org/10.16497/j.cnki.1672-335x.20150916.004.

146. Yang, Z. J., & Guo, J. F. (2017). 北极生态安全对中国的影响及应对研究— 基于非传统安全视角 [The impact of Arctic ecological security on China and China's response from the perspective of non-traditional security]. *辽宁大学学报（哲学社会科学版） [Journal of Liaoning University (Philosophy and Social Sciences)], 45*(6), 143-150. https://doi.org/10.16197/j.cnki.lnupse.2017.06.018.

147. Young, O. R. (2011). The future of the Arctic: Cauldron of conflict or zone of peace? *International Affairs, 87*(1), 185-193. https://www.jstor.org/stable/20869618.

148. Yu, X. F., & Xie, G. P. (2015). "选择性"再建构:安全化理论的新拓展 ["Selectively" Reconstruction: a new expansion of security theory]. *世界经济与政治 [World Economy and Politics]*, (9), 104-121.

149. Zhang, H. B. (2010). *气候变化与中国国家安全 [Climate change and China's national security]*. 时事出版社 [Current Affair Press].

150. Zhang, S. J., & Li, X. (2010). 中国能源安全与中国北极战略定位 [China's energy security and China's strategic positioning of the Arctic]. *国际观察 [International Review]*, (4), 64-71.

151. Zhang, W. M. (2017). *气候变迁与中华国运 [Climate change and China's Destiny]*. 海洋出版社 [China Ocean Press].

152. Zhang, X. D. (2017, December 11). "冰上丝路"见证中俄合作新成果 [The "Polar Silk Road" witnesses new achievements of Sino-Russian cooperation]. 人民日报 [People's Daily]. http://world.people.com.cn/n1/2017/1211/c1002-29697384.html.

153. Zhang, Y. (2017, December 10). 全球最大北极液化天然气项目："冰上丝绸之路"启航 [The world's largest Arctic LNG project: The "Polar Silk Road" sets sail]. 光明日报 [Guangming Daily]. https://www.sohu.com/a/209536628_162758.

154. Zhang, Z. X. (2013). 中国在全球搜寻能源安全：为何利益如此攸关 [China's global search for energy security: why energy interests are so crucial]. In McKay, H., & Song, L. G. (Eds.), 中国经济再平衡与可持续增长 [The rebalance and sustainable growth of China's economy] (pp. 305-329). 社会科学文献出版社 [Social Sciences Academic Press].

ASSESSING THE IMPACT OF DISASTERS ON TECHNOLOGY TRANSFER UNDER INTERNATIONAL ECONOMIC LAW: THE CASE OF SPACE-BASED TECHNOLOGIES

Federica Cristani

Abstract: This chapter focuses on the economic consequences of natural disasters for affected states, in particular as regards technology transfer, taking space-based technology transfer in the Arctic region as a case-study. Space-based technology have indeed become an important element of regional, national and local disaster risk reduction strategies: suffice to recall, among others, the use of remote sensing and geographic information systems tools for monitoring and mapping risks, as well as the role of space technology applications in early warning and monitoring of slow onset disasters. But what happens in case of transfer of space-based technologies? Do disasters impact such processes and which (international) instruments come into play? And what is the current situation in the Arctic region? This chapter examines the relevant regulatory framework of reference at the international level, with a mapping of technology transfer provisions in international disaster law instruments, international economic law provisions on technology transfer applicable in the context of disaster-related situations and space law provisions applying in case of transfer of space-based technologies, with a special focus on the Arctic.

Keywords: natural disasters, space-based technology transfer, international economic law, international disaster law, Arctic

How natural disasters affect (space-based) technology transfer: a preliminary overview

Natural disasters may have devastating impacts on human life, as well as on the economy and environment of the affected states: during the last World Trade Organization's Ministerial Conference in Buenos Aires (10-13 December 2017), several states, especially from the Caribbean Community and Common Market (CARICOM) and the Group of Small and Vulnerable Economies (SVEs) stressed out the impact of disasters on their economies: the governmental representative of Saint Lucia (speaking on behalf of CARICOM), pointed out that "[…] many small and vulnerable economies in the Caribbean […] suffered massive devastation and absolute destruction of critical infrastructure from […] hurricanes […M]any of these countries are faced with the herculean task of reconstructing their entire economies" (Saint Lucia, 2017), as echoed by, among others, the statement of the governmental representative of Guatemala (speaking on behalf of SVEs), who highlighted "the need for special consideration and targeted assistance to be given to SVEs, inter alia, in the areas of Aid for Trade, Trade and Transfer of Technology; Trade Facilitation, Trade Finance and Development Assistance which are priorities for special consideration by the WTO" (Guatemala, 2017).

In this context, space-based technology applications have become an important element of regional, national and local disaster risk reduction strategies: we can briefly recall, among others, the use of remote sensing and geographic information systems tools for monitoring and mapping risks, the use of earth observation products for humanitarian assistance and damage and needs assessment, the use of space technology for earthquake damage assessment and earthquake relief, as well as the role of space technology applications in early warning and monitoring of slow onset disasters. While space-based technologies have been applied in manifold situations and regions around the world, they have proved to be particularly useful in the Arctic, a challenging region where to live and work, with vast distances and difficult weather conditions; in such context, space-based technologies can help, e.g., in reaching remote areas that could not be accessed in any other way.

But what happens in case of transfer of space-based technologies? Do disasters impact such processes and which (international) instruments come into play? And what is the current situation in the Arctic region? These are the questions that this Chapter will cover in the next paragraphs. Before entering into the question of the transfer of space-based technologies in the context of disasters, we should question what we mean by ´disasters´ under international law.

The United Nations (UN) *Open-ended intergovernmental expert working group on indicators and terminology relating to disaster risk reduction* (established by the UN General Assembly Resolution 69/284 of 25 June 2015) has defined *disaster* as a "serious disruption of the functioning of a community or a society at any scale due to hazardous events interacting with conditions of exposure, vulnerability and capacity, leading to one or more of the following: human, material, economic and environmental losses and impacts" (UN, 2016).

For the scope of this Chapter, we focus on *natural* disasters, arising from geological or geophysical hazards, such as earthquakes, and hydro-meteorological hazards, such as droughts and flooding.

The economic consequences of natural disasters affect all aspects of economy: imports play a critical role in recovery and reconstruction - the more severe the damage inflicted by a natural disaster, the broader the range of different goods and services that may need to be imported (WTO, 2019, p. 5); on the other hand, natural disasters can have a negative effect on exports – especially agricultural exports usually take the longest time to recover following hydrometeorological disasters; furthermore, disasters generally create debt, with governments borrowing to finance recovery and reconstruction (WTO, 2020).

When talking about the impact of disasters on the economy of affected countries, we should note that the relevant figures and data are quite sparse, especially when it comes to smaller-scale disasters. Moreover, it should be taken into account that other crises or challenges may occur in disaster-affected states, thus making the measurement of natural disaster effects more complicated to be assessed; e.g., migration or economic shocks often intertwine with disasters – e.g. a World Trade Organization (WTO) report highlighted how the drought conditions in Paraguay of 2011-2012 caused a contraction in economic output of equivalent size to that of the global economic crisis just two years before (WTO, 2020).

Overall, the lack of precise and disaggregated data on the impact of natural disasters on the economy of affected countries makes it more difficult to assess the situation and, consequently, to identify the appropriate legislative and political measures that should be adopted.

In 2018, the WTO undertook a research looking into the impact of natural disasters on trade, which resulted in two comprehensive studies: the first one examines the economic and trade impact of natural disasters, with a particular focus on six disaster-affected countries (Dominica, Fiji, Nepal, Saint Lucia, Tonga and Vanuatu); the second one includes a legal mapping of the measures that governments can take under WTO agreements in the context of disaster situations (WTO, 2020).

This chapter takes stock of the WTO research and goes beyond it by exploring the impacts of disasters on technology transfer – which has been only partially covered by the above-mentioned research. The focus of the analysis will be on space-based technology transfer, with a particular insight on the situation in the Arctic region.

The following paragraphs offer a general overview of the regulatory framework in place when it comes to technology transfer in the context of natural disasters; then, they zoom in on space-based technology transfer, with a particular focus on the Arctic region.

Technology transfer in the context of disasters: assessing the current regulatory framework at the international level

When talking about 'technology transfer' we refer to the definition provided by the United Nations Conference on Trade and Development (UNCTAD), which in turn referred to the one adopted by the World Intellectual Property Organization (WIPO), according to which "[t]ransfer of technology may be understood […] as […] a series of processes for sharing ideas, knowledge, technology and skills with another individual or institution (e.g. a company, a university or a governmental body) and of acquisition by the other of such ideas, knowledge, technologies and skills […] Thus, "knowledge" is at the core of the notion of technology transfer. It could be embodied in hardware such as in plant, machinery and equipment or disembodied in the form of patents, know-how, trademarks, designs and licences in general. Similarly, technology can be described as "codified" – that is, it is contained in written documents or registered designs – or "uncodified", such as human skills and know-how […]" (UNCTAD, 2012, p. 4; see also WIPO, 2011).

As regards more in particular the process of the actual transfer of technology, UNCTAD states that "[t]echnology transfer can be governed by explicit contractual arrangements, such as licensing between business partners, but it can also be managed implicitly through the establishment of subsidiaries and affiliates of transnational corporations (TNCs) in other countries […] Technology transfer transactions may include not only the assignment, sale and licensing of industrial property, but also related know-how and technical expertise embodied in, for example, models, instructions or guides" (UNCTAD, 2012, p. 6).

Technology transfer can be affected by disasters in different way: on the one hand, import of technology (e.g. information technology equipment and products that can be also used in the disaster relief effort) can be subject to customs clearance delays because of the natural disaster (WTO, 2020), e.g., a report by the International Federation of Red Cross and Red Crescent Societies (IFRC) on Nepal observed that while satellite phone technology would have been extremely useful for communicating in times of disaster, it was very costly and had not been granted any tax, licensing or import exemptions, which placed it out of reach of most relief providers; moreover, when disaster-affected countries participate in global value chains, disasters can have an impact across these supply networks – e.g. flooding in Thailand and the earthquake and tsunami in Japan in 2011 had a major impact on global production networks for cars and electronic products (IFRC, 2014).

On the other hand, technology transfer can be crucial in the recovery phase: actually, the need to rebuild roads, railways, ports, infrastructures after a disaster are often fulfilled by imports of construction services and transfer of technology and know-how from foreign construction companies with the aim to "build back better" and reduce future exposure to (natural or man-made) hazards (WTO, 2019, p. 20).

When it comes to assess the relevant regulatory framework of reference at the international level and identify which international rules apply in such situations, the picture is quite fragmented. On the one hand, we find some provisions in international disaster law-related instruments; on the other hand, we have some provisions in international economic law instruments dealing with technology transfer that can apply in the context of disaster situations. The fragmentation is increased by the fact that, as noted by UNCTAD, "data on international [technology transfer] is relatively scarce"; accordingly, "it is difficult to establish an accurate indication of the geographical distribution of international flows of technology" (UNCTAD, 2012, p. 30).

The following paragraphs overview which are the most relevant technology transfer provisions which are included international disaster law instruments, on the one hand, and which are the most relevant international economic law provisions on technology transfer which are applicable in the context of disaster-related situations, on the other.

Technology transfer provisions in international disaster law instruments

Under international disaster law, we find relevant treaties that include a number of provisions on the entry of foreign relief goods, equipment (which can be relevant also for transfer of technology) and personnel in a disaster affected country (Adinolfi, 2021, p. 8; Fisher, 2003, p. 24). The relevant regulatory picture is rather fragmented: the scope of such treaties may vary, covering either any disaster or some typologies or specific events (e.g. the Convention on Assistance in Case of Nuclear Accident or Radiological Emergency, concluded in 1986 after the Chernobyl nuclear accident); moreover, commitments and obligations may regard a restricted range of goods (e.g., the 1998 Tampere Convention on the Provision of Telecommunication Resources for Disaster Mitigation and Relief Operations or the 1990 Istanbul Convention on Temporary Admission, for equipment covering only medical, surgical and laboratory devices). A key instrument was adopted in March 2015 by the UN World Conference on Disaster Risk Reduction, namely the Sendai Framework on Disaster Risk Reduction 2015–2030, later endorsed by the UN General Assembly (UN, 2015). The Sendai Framework makes no direct reference to trade policy as an instrument to address disaster preparedness. However, a trade component of resilience strategies can be inferred from some of the suggested actions: states are indeed recommended to establish coherent laws and regulations that can be effectively implemented in the event of a disaster, which may include, for example, trade-related regulations on customs tariffs or customs processes and procedures applied on the entry of foreign relief goods and equipment (Adinolfi, 2021, p. 9).

The Sendai Framework includes also specific provisions on technology transfer: under "Priority 1: Understanding disaster risk", it states that "[…] it is important [t]o promote and enhance, through international cooperation, including technology transfer, access to and the sharing and use of non-sensitive data and information […]" (Sendai Framework, para. 25, lit. c); furthermore, under Section VI (International cooperation and global partnership) it states that "[i]n addressing economic disparity and disparity in technological innovation […] among countries, it is crucial to enhance technology transfer, involving a process of enabling and facilitating flows of skill, knowledge, ideas, know-how and technology from developed to developing countries" (Sendai Framework, para. 40), recalling also that "[…] public and private transfer of reliable, affordable, appropriate and modern environmentally sound technology, on concessional and preferential terms [...] are critically important means of reducing disaster risk" (Sendai Framework, para. 46).

One year later, in 2016, the UN International Law Commission (ILC) adopted the Draft Articles on the Protection of Persons in the Event of Disasters (UN ILC, 2016), which includes some provisions that can be relevant also in the context of technology transfer: article 9 (1) of the Draft Articles on the Protection of Persons in the Event of Disasters sets a general duty to take "appropriate measures, including through legislation and regulations, to prevent, mitigate, and prepare for disaster"; one may argue that such 'measures' might be also of economic nature. Moreover, once established a general duty to cooperate in the event of a disaster (article 7), the ILC identified specific areas in which cooperation may be suitable, including the provision of "relief personnel, equipment and goods, and scientific, medical and technical resources" (article 8); the ILC also stressed that "forms of cooperation not specified in the present draft article are not excluded, such as: financial support; *technology transfer* covering, among others, technology relating to satellite imagery; training; information-sharing; joint simulation exercises and planning; and undertaking needs assessments and situation overview" [emphasis added] (paragraph 4 of the commentary to article 8).

Another key document is the Model Act for the Facilitation and Regulation of International Disaster Relief and Initial Recovery Assistance adopted by the International Federation of Red Cross and Red Crescent Societies (IFRC) in 2013 (IFRC, 2013), which suggests a detailed discipline to be adopted at the national level in order to cope with hazards. The Model Act, in particular, advocates the exemption from customs duties and other taxes on the entry of the relief material (article 32). Moreover, article 43 allows "to re-export any Equipment or unused Goods and to do so without the imposition of any taxes, export duties, or similar charge", and the commentary makes it clear that "[t]hese provisions apply both to unused Goods and Equipment, and particularly to vehicles and other types of equipment that an Eligible Actor might need for use while providing International Disaster Assistance, but would then wish to take out of the affected state for use elsewhere. For example, electricity generators, large-scale water purifying equipment, mobile medical facilities, telecommunications and information technology equipment" (Adinolfi, 2021, p. 10). This can also apply in the context of technology transfer.

Generally, it seems that disaster-related international instruments suggest the possibility to waive from custom duties when it comes to transfer "equipment" – which can be understood also as including technology transfer. Such tendency is confirmed also at the regional level – e.g. the Council of Europe's 1960 Agreement on the Temporary Importation, free of duty, of Medical, Surgical and Laboratory Equipment for use on free loan in Hospitals and other Medical Institutions for purposes of Diagnosis or Treatment aims to enable countries in urgent need to obtain the necessary material (according to article 2, limited to "medical, surgical and laboratory equipment for use in hospitals and other medical institutions") free from customs duties for a renewable period of six months, especially in the event of an epidemic or a catastrophe (Council of Europe, 1960); also article 10 of the Agreement among the Governments of the Participating States of the Black Sea Economic Cooperation (BSEC) on collaboration in Emergency Assistance and Emergency Response to natural and man-made Disasters states that "[…] Equipment and Goods of assistance exported and imported for Assistance pursuant to the present Agreement shall be exempt from customs duties, taxes and fees […]" (BSEC, 1998).

International economic law provisions on technology transfer applicable in the context of disaster-related situations

WTO´s Agreements include a few provisions expressly taking into consideration disaster events: we can recall article XVIII of the 1994 General Agreement on Tariffs and Trade (GATT) and the relevant Interpretative Notes, according to which WTO developing Members may adopt measures affecting imports or modify or withdraw scheduled tariff concessions in order also to promote "the reconstruction of an industry destroyed or substantially damaged as a result of hostilities or natural disasters" (WTO, 1994, p. 492). This clause has been invoked in 2002, when Bangladesh justified the notified measure on the ground of its exposure to periodic flooding and cyclones (WTO, Council for Trade in Goods, 2002, para. 4).

The above-mentioned WTO report on the impact of natural disasters on trade make reference to trade measures adopted in the context of (1) disaster response, in the immediate aftermath of a disaster event, (2) disaster recovery and (3) disaster resilience, with a view to support the ability of an economy to face future shocks derived from natural hazards (Adinolfi, 2019, p. 5).

More in particular, the WTO report underlines that in the (1) disaster response phase, trade measures taken by a disaster-affected country are mainly focused on facilitating the availability of domestic and foreign relief goods, equipment, services and personnel (Adinolfi, 2019, p. 6). As regards (2) disaster recovery, the focus is more on subsidies that can be claimed by disaster-affected Members and tariff protection that can be accorded to badly affected businesses or sectors (Adinolfi, 2019, p. 6). At the same time, recovery is likely to be accelerated by market opening as for example concerns the importation of products necessary for the reconstruction of physical infrastructure, e.g. building materials (Adinolfi, 2019, p. 6). As regards (3) disaster resilience, it has been stressed that liberalization of some services (e.g. health services, engineering services, telecommunication and weather-related services) could have a positive impact, encouraging the growth of the private sector and, overall, enhancing the domestic capacity to supply services crucial for reducing vulnerability to disasters. Moreover, trade partners can play a crucial role in providing technical assistance to disaster-affected countries (Adinolfi, 2019, p. 7).

And what about technology transfer? A number of provisions in the WTO agreements mention the need for a transfer of technology to take place between developed and developing countries. However, it is not clear how such a transfer takes place in practice and if specific measures might be taken within the WTO to encourage such flows of technology, and, more in particular, how such provisions apply in the context of disaster (WTO, 2001). As recalled by UNCTAD, technology transfer may take place through different channels, including foreign direct investment and trade flows of technological or technology related goods and services (UNCTAD, 2012, p. 25); accordingly, relevant provisions can be found in different international instruments dealing with international economic relations, e.g. trade in goods, investment and licensing (UNCTAD, 2012, p. 86). We can count several international, regional and bilateral agreements containing measures related to transfer of technology; the relevant provisions follow different approaches, depending on the object and purpose of the respective agreement: we can recall, for example, the 1883 Paris Convention for the Protection of Industrial Property and the 1994 WTO Agreement on Trade-Related Aspects of Intellectual Property Rights (TRIPS Agreement) – dealing with certain aspect of transfer of intellectual property rights – or the 1985 Vienna Convention for the Protection of the Ozone Layer – where the parties agreed to cooperate in the development and transfer of technology; at the regional level, we can mention the 2014 Association Agreement between European Union and Ukraine and the 2020 United States-Mexico-Canada Agreement – both referring to the transfer of intellectual property rights - or the 1986 Agreement on ASEAN Energy Cooperation – specifically including provisions on transfer of technology in energy-related activities; when it comes to the bilateral level, worth mentioning are, among others, the 2001 Kuwait - Netherlands Bilateral Investment Agreement – encouraging the transfer of technology through foreign direct investment - or the 2003 Agreement on Scientific and Technological Cooperation between the United States of America and Bangladesh – expressly devoted to cooperation on technology transfer (UNCTAD, 2001). Overall, such agreements tend to promote access to technologies and, in some cases, the development of local capabilities in developing countries, particularly in least developed countries (UNCTAD, 2001).

This regulatory fragmentation makes it more complicated to identify the provisions to apply in the context of disasters; in any case, the link between technology transfer and disaster is very relevant, as stressed by the representative of Bangladesh at the WTO Fourth Symposium on natural disasters and trade that was held on 29 November 2019, who recalled the complementarity of technology transfer for disaster risk management in the context of the WTO TRIPS Agreement, and proposed to apply article 66 of TRIPS also in the context of disasters, according to which "[d]eveloped country Members shall provide incentives to enterprises and institutions in their territories for the purpose of promoting and encouraging technology transfer to least-developed country Members in order to enable them to create a sound and viable technological base" (WTO, 2019, p. 225).

One important reference, as regards post-disaster situation, can be made to the WTO Trade Facilitation Agreement (TFA) – which entered into force on 22 February 2017, and has been accepted so far by 151 WTO Members -, whose provisions are aimed to facilitate the entry of equipment necessary for relief operations. The notion of "equipment" is generally referred to items that are not destined for immediate consumption and not donated to local authorities. For instance, vehicles, medical or telecommunication devices could come under this definition (Adinolfi, 2021, p. 19).

Overall, provisions on technology transfer in international economic instruments tend to promote access to technologies and, in some cases, the development of local capabilities in developing countries, particularly in least developed countries.

Transfer of space-based technologies in the context of disasters

The provisions we have overviewed in the previous paragraphs on technology transfers in both international disaster law instruments and in international economic agreements are applicable also to the transfer of space-based technology. However, when we talk about space-based technologies, also a number of specificities should be taken into consideration.

As already mentioned, space-based technologies can have a crucial role in the context of disaster risk reduction strategies. As the United Nations Committee on the Peaceful Uses of Outer Space (COPUOS) - established as an ad hoc United Nations (UN) Committee by the UN General Assembly with Resolutions 1348 (XIII) of 13 December 1958 and Resolution 1472 (XIV) of 12 December 1959 with the task to promote international cooperation in the exploration of outer space – has recently pointed out is its 2021 Report (COPUOS, 2021), "[t]he Committee noted the importance of space-based information for disaster management and emergency response, utilizing remote sensing data and Earth observation satellites for developing multi-hazard early warning systems and disaster impact analysis for all types of natural disasters […]" (COPUOS, 2021, para. 95). Also the Sendai Framework for Disaster Risk Reduction restates the importance of satellite observations in the context of disaster prevention and management, making it clear that "[…] it is important […] to develop, periodically update and disseminate, as appropriate, location-based disaster risk information, including risk maps […] by using, as applicable, geospatial information technology" (COPUOS, 2021, para. 24). Indeed, remotely sensed images can provide information on the earth's surface and enable the monitoring of the land structure in relation to, e.g., flooding patterns or of the composition of snow in relation to avalanches; on the other hand, when a disaster has already occurred, remotely sensed images can be used to organize rescue operations (ESCAP, 2013, p. 3).

However, as the 2021 COPUOS Report restated, a number of challenges exist for space-based technology transfer, especially for developing countries: the Report highlighted that there is indeed "a significant divide between countries that had made great progress in technological development in space matters and those working to create or strengthen the sector, which was why it was necessary to further promote […] technology transfer […]" (COPUOS, 2021, para. 250) and that "[…] particular attention should be given to […] enabling technology transfer to enable countries to develop local solutions to global problems" (COPUOS, 2021, para. 329). This is also in line with the Sendai Framework for Disaster Risk Reduction, according to which "[…] it is important […] to promote and enhance, through international cooperation, including technology transfer, access to and the sharing and use of […] space-based technologies and related services" (Sendai Framework for Disaster Risk Reduction 2015 – 2030, para. 25, lit. c).

In the space sector, technology transfer is generally known as "spin-off"; a number of space agencies - e.g. the National Aeronautics and Space Administration (NASA), the Canadian Space Agency and the German Aerospace Center) define as "spin-offs" those "technologies initially created to meet the agency's objectives, which incorporated internal expertise, and then […] commercialised as a product or service to serve other uses outside of the agency" (OECD, 2021, p. 14). Spin-offs may occur through different channels, including (1) collaborative research through participation by e.g. academia or private firms in government-led programs and projects, (2) commercialization of government intellectual property, typically through the licensing of patents or firm creation, or through (3) other channels, such as labor mobility or facility sharing (OECD, 2021, p. 10). Space-based technology transfers may follow formal channels, which normally involve detailed transactions between the research and the industry counterparts, or informal channels, with less traceable agreements among the parts involved – e.g. in the form of tacit transfers (OECD, 2021, p.19). The latter channels makes it more difficult to obtain complete and accurate data about spin-offs.

Overall, patenting and licensing are the most common channels adopted by space agencies and technology transfer offices to promote the commercialization of inventions: in this respect, we can recall that NASA's patent portfolio contains more than 1 200 patents that are available for different types of exclusive and non-exclusive licenses fees, while the European Space Agency (ESA) patents between ten and twenty inventions every year (OECD, 2021, p. 23). License agreements are different within space agencies: NASA, usually negotiates licenses case by case (NASA, 2019), while ESA generally grant licenses to be used in the frame of ESA contracts, or for privately-funded activities (ESA, 2021). Space-based technology transfer can be a complex process (Hertzfeld, 2002, p. 308), and especially developing countries still encounter difficulties in accessing the relevant technologies and data.

In this respect, international cooperation is key in ensuring technology transfer, as clearly pointed out in the UN General Assembly Resolution 51/122 of 13 December 1996 (*Declaration on International Cooperation in the Exploration and Use of Outer Space for the Benefit and in the Interest of All States, Taking into Particular Account the Needs of Developing Countries*), according to which "[i]nternational cooperation, while taking into particular account the needs of developing countries, should aim […] at […f]acilitating the exchange of expertise and technology among States on a mutually acceptable basis" (UNGA, 1996: para. 5). And already in 1986, the UN General Assembly recognized that data obtained with the use of space-based technologies should be accessible by al countries: in its Resolution 41/65 of 3 December 1986 on *Principles Relating to Remote Sensing of the Earth from Outer Space*, it expressly stated that "[…] States participating in remote sensing activities that have identified processed data and analyzed information in their possession that may be useful to States affected by natural disasters, or likely to be affected by impeding natural disasters, shall transmit such data and information to States concerned as promptly as possible" (Principle XI).

This is in line with Article 1 of the Outer Space Treaty (UN, 1967), according to which "[t]he exploration and use of outer space […] shall be carried out for the benefit and in the interests of all countries, irrespective of their degree of economic or scientific development […]".

To date, a number of international and regional platforms already exist with the aim to foster cooperation among countries in the use of space-based technologies in the context of disasters, like the United Nations Platform for Space-based Information for Disaster Management and Emergency Response (UN-SPIDER) - established by the UN General Assembly with Resolution 61/110 of 14 December 2006 and implemented through the United Nations Office for Outer Space Affairs (OOSA) -, which serves as a "platform for information, communication and process support that fostered the exchange of information, the sharing of experiences, capacity-building and technical advisory support and services" (COPUOS, 2021, para. 96).

Worth recalling are also, among others, the Charter on Cooperation to Achieve the Coordinated Use of Space Facilities in the Event of Natural or Technological Disasters (the so-called International Charter on Space and Major Disasters), a worldwide collaboration established in 2000 among space agencies with the aim to make satellite-derived information and products available in order to support disaster response efforts (The International Charter Space and Major Disasters, 2000), and the Recovery Observatory of the Committee on Earth Observation Satellites, which aims at collecting and making available satellite data to be used in situations of recovery from natural disasters (UN-SPIDER, 2020; Zannoni, 2021).

At the European level, worth mentioning is the Copernicus Emergency Management Service (EMS) - regulated by the Europen Union Regulation 377/2014 -, which makes geospatial information derived from satellite remote sensing available to all relevant stakeholders that are involved in the management of disasters (UN-SPIDER, 2012; Zannoni, 2021).

These kinds of international and regional cooperation platforms are crucial in enabling countries to access and use space-based information, also in the context of disasters (ESCAP, 2013, p. 20).

A focus on the Arctic region: using space-based technologies in the context of disasters

The Arctic is a challenging region where to live and work; in this respect, space-based technologies are extremely important (Wilson Center, 2018). Indeed, space information can help in in detecting and forecasting natural hazards that are difficult to detect from observations made from the sparse network of polar stations (Arctic.ru, 2015); satellites can oversee remote areas in the region that could not be accessed in any other way; communications satellites can also bring communities across the Arctic and around the world closer together; and earth observation satellites can monitor pollution and environmental change (Polar View, 2012, p. 3).

It its 2019 conclusions on "Space solutions for a sustainable Arctic", the Council of the European Union made it clear that "[e]arth observation, satellite navigation, satellite communications, and space weather observations covering the Arctic already contribute to or have the potential of contributing to addressing the challenges in the region" (Council of the European Union, 2019, para. 2); at the same time it "notes that availability of continuous satellite communications capacity in the Arctic still has gaps" (Council of the European Union, 2019, para. 12).

At the European level, the EU Satellite Centre (SatCen) - founded in 1992 as a Western European Union body and incorporated as an agency into the EU in 2002 (European Union Satellite Centre, 2021) - offers geospatial analysis that support the EU's efforts to monitor the security situation in the Arctic region, while Galileo – the EU's global navigation satellite system established as a joint initiative of the European Commission and ESA (ESA, 2021) - is already offering search and rescue services. Also the above mentioned EU's Copernicus Emergency Management Service offers monitoring, early warning and mapping in the Arctic (European Commission, High Representative of the Union for Foreign Affairs and Security Policy, 2021, pp. 3, 5).

What is a peculiar feature in the Arctic, is the cooperation in space-based technology transfer among all the relevant stakeholders, especially between public and private actors.

In this respect, we can briefly recall, within the framework of the Arctic Council, the work of the Task Force on Improved Connectivity in the Arctic, established in 2017 with the aim to overview technological solutions, commercial opportunities and industry best practices in the Arctic. Worth mentioning are in particular its efforts in engaging with the telecommunications industry, also for the use of space-based technologies; during its meeting, the Task Force regularly invites representatives from business entities, different authorities, stakeholders and various organizations to present their perspectives on the challenges of connectivity in the Arctic. This allows a better understanding of the technologies that current exist and/or are being developed (Arctic Council, 2019, p. 9).

As a recent example of recent cooperation, we can recall the contract signed in March 2021 between ESA and OHB Sweden, Swedish space systems provider, for contracting a prototype satellite by 2024 that would gather Arctic weather data and would provide important information for climate research and disaster management (UN-SPIDER, 2021).

Some concluding remarks

As the previous paragraphs have shown, the international regulatory framework of technology transfer in the context of disaster is quite fragmented, with provisions coming from both international disaster and international economic law sectors. When it comes to space-based technology, the picture becomes more complicated, due, among others, to additional space-related instruments that come into play and the involvement of space agencies and their different rules on, for example, licensing.

Overall, the legal instruments at stake do not seem to put much emphasis on some core questions related to (space-based) technology transfer in times of disasters – e.g. whether special conditions apply in the case of the need to use (space-based) technology by disaster-affected countries. In this respect, further research is needed in order to develop a comprehensive framework of reference on the issues at stake.

In this regard, the Arctic region seems to provide a positive example of international and regional cooperation in the use of space-based technologies – also in the context of disaster management, even though regulatory gaps still exist on how to deal with technology transfer. One of the main challenges in this respect is the lack of evidence on transfer and commercialization of space-based technologies. As also pointed out in the 2021 OECD Report on "Space technology transfers and their commercialisation", more efforts are still needed in order to improve the tracking of operations related to technological transfers (OECD 2021, p. 40). This would lead to a better and comprehesive understanding of the relevant issues and to the definition of well-suited regulatory instruments.

References

1. Adinolfi, G. (2019). *Natural Disasters and Trade. Research Study II. A legal mapping. Executive Summary.* World Trade Organization. https://www.wto.org/english/tratop_e/devel_e/study2_sympnaturaldisaster29112019_e.pdf.
2. Adinolfi, G. (2021). Strengthening Resilience to Disasters through International Trade Law: the Role of WTO Agreements on Trade in Goods. *Yearbook of International Disaster Law*, 2(1), 1–37. https://doi.org/10.1163/26662531_00201_002.
3. Arctic.ru (2015, November 5). *Arctic research project zeros in on natural hazards.* Arctic.ru – Analysis. https://arctic.ru/analitic/20151105/219066.html.
4. Arctic Council, Task Force on Improved Connectivity in the Arctic (2019, May 7). *Report. Improving connectivity in the Arctic.* https://www.uarctic.org/news/2019/5/task-force-on-improved-connectivity-in-the-arctic-tfica-report-improving-connectivity-in-the-arctic.
5. BSEC [Black Sea Economic Cooperation] (1998, April 15). Agreement among the Governments of the Participating States of the Black Sea Economic Cooperation (BSEC) on collaboration in Emergency Assistance and Emergency Response to natural and man-made Disasters. http://www.bsec-organization.org/charter.

6. Council of the European Union (2019, November 21). *Council conclusions on "Space solutions for a sustainable Arctic"*, 13996/19. https://www.consilium.europa.eu/en/press/press-releases/2019/11/29/space-solutions-for-a-sustainable-arctic-council-adopts-conclusions/#.
7. COPUOS [UN on the Peaceful Uses of Outer Space] (2021, September 13). *Report of the Committee on the Peaceful Uses of Outer Space. Sixty-fourth session (25 August–3 September 2021)*, A/76/20. https://www.unoosa.org/oosa/documents-and-resolutions/search.jspx.
8. Council of Europe (1960, April 28) Agreement on the Temporary Importation, free of duty, of Medical, Surgical and Laboratory Equipment for use on free loan in Hospitals and other Medical Institutions for purposes of Diagnosis or Treatment, ETS No. 033. https://www.coe.int/en/web/conventions/full-list/-/conventions/treaty/033.
9. ESA [European Space Agency] (2021). *Licensing*. https://www.esa.int/Enabling_Support/Space_Engineering_Technology/Microelectronics/Licensing.
10. ESCAP [Economic and Social Commission for Asia and the Pacific] (2013, December). Sound practices in space technology applications for disaster risk reduction and inclusive and sustainable development. *ESCAP Technical Paper*. https://repository.unescap.org/handle/20.500.12870/3097.
11. ESA [European Space Agency] (2021). *What is Galileo?*. https://www.esa.int/Applications/Navigation/Galileo/What_is_Galileo.
12. European Commission, High Representative of the Union for Foreign Affairs and Security Policy (2021, October 13). *Joint Communication. A stronger EU engagement for a peaceful, sustainable and prosperous Arctic*, JOIN(2021) 27 final. https://eeas.europa.eu/headquarters/headquarters-homepage/105481/joint-communication-stronger-eu-engagement-peaceful-sustainable-and-prosperous-arctic_en.

13. European Union Satellite Centre (2021). *The Centre*. https://www.satcen.europa.eu/page/the_centre.
14. Fisher, H. (2003). International disaster response law treaties: trends, patterns and lacunae. In IFRC [International Federation of Red Cross and Red Crescent Societies] (Ed.), *International disaster response law, principles and practices: reflections, prospects and challenges* (pp. 24-44). International Federation of Red Cross and Red Crescent Societies.
15. Guatemala (2017, December 10-13). *Statement at the plenary session of the Ministerial Conference, Eleventh Session*. https://www.wto.org/english/thewto_e/minist_e/mc11_e/mc11_plenary_e.htm.
16. Hertzfeld, H.R. (2002). Technology transfer in the space sector: an international perspective. *The Journal of Technology Transfer*, 27(4), 307-309. http://dx.doi.org/10.1023/A:1020222521994.
17. IFRC [International Federation of Red Cross and Red Crescent Societies] (2013, March). Model Act for the Facilitation and Regulation of International Disaster Relief and Initial Recovery Assistance. http://archive.ipu.org/PDF/publications/act-en.pdf.
18. IFRC, "Regulatory barriers to providing emergency and transitional shelter after disasters Country case study: Nepal", IFRC, 2014, http://flagship2.nrrc.org.np/regulatory-barriers-providing-emergency-and-transitional-shelter-after-disasters-country-case-study.
19. NASA [National Aeronautics and Space Administration], Office of Inspector General (2019, April 15). *NASA's technology transfer process*. Report No. IG-19-016. https://oig.nasa.gov/docs/IG-19-016.pdf.
20. OECD [Organisation for Economic Co-operation and Development] (2021, July). Space technology transfers and their commercialization. *OECD Science, Technology and Industry*

Policy Papers, No. 116. https://www.oecd-ilibrary.org/science-and-technology/space-technology-transfers-and-their-commercialisation_0e78ff9f-en.
21. Polar View (2012, March). *The Contribution of Space Technologies to Arctic Policy Priorities. Executive Summary.* https://www.esa.int/Enabling_Support/Preparing_for_the_Future/Discovery_and_Preparation/The_Contribution_of_Space_Technologies_to_Arctic_Policy_Priorities.
22. Saint Lucia (2017, December 10-13). *Statement at the plenary session of the Ministerial Conference, Eleventh Session.* https://www.wto.org/english/thewto_e/minist_e/mc11_e/mc11_plenary_e.htm.
23. The International Charter Space and Major Disasters (2000). Charter On Cooperation To Achieve The Coordinated Use Of Space Facilities In The Event Of Natural Or Technological Disasters, Rev.3 (25/4/2000).2. https://disasterscharter.org/web/guest/text-of-the-charter.
24. UN [United Nations] (1967, January 25). Treaty on Principles Governing the Activities of States in the Exploration and Use of Outer Space, including the Moon and Other Celestial Bodies. https://www.unoosa.org/oosa/en/ourwork/spacelaw/treaties/introouterspacetreaty.html.
25. UN (2015, June 3). Sendai Framework on Disaster Risk Reduction 2015–2020, A/RES/69/283. https://www.undrr.org/publication/sendai-framework-disaster-risk-reduction-2015-2030#:~:text=The%20Sendai%20Framework%20for%20Disaster,Investing%20in%20disaster%20reduction%20for.
26. UN (2016, December 1). *Report of the open-ended intergovernmental expert working group on indicators and terminology relating to disaster risk reduction*, A/71/644. https://www.undrr.org/publication/report-open-ended-intergovernmental-expert-working-group-indicators-and-terminology.

27. UNCTAD [United Nations Conference on Trade and Development] (2001). *Compendium of International Arrangements on Transfer of Technology. Selected Instruments*, UNCTAD/ITE/IPC/Misc.5. https://unctad.org/system/files/official-document/psiteipcm5.en.pdf.
28. UNCTAD (2012). *Virtual Institute Teaching Material on Transfer of Technology.* https://vi.unctad.org/resources-mainmenu-64/teaching-materials-mainmenu-65/151-vi-teaching-material-on-transfer-of-technology.
29. UNGA [UN General Assembly] (1996, December 13). *Resolution, Declaration on International Cooperation in the Exploration and Use of Outer Space for the Benefit and in the Interest of All States, Taking into Particular Account the Needs of Developing Countries*, A/RES/51/122. https://www.unoosa.org/oosa/en/ourwork/spacelaw/principles/space-benefits-declaration.html.
30. UN ILC [UN International Law Commission] (2016). Draft articles on the protection of persons in the event of disasters, with commentaries. *Yearbook of the International Law Commission*, Vol. II, Part Two. https://legal.un.org/ilc/guide/6_3.shtml.
31. UN-SPIDER (2000). *International Charter Space and Major Disasters.* https://www.un-spider.org/international-charter-space-and-major-disasters.
32. UN-SPIDER (2012). *Copernicus Emergency Management Service (EMS)*. https://www.un-spider.org/copernicus-emergency-management-service-ems.
33. UN-SPIDER (2021, March 30). ESA and OHB Sweden sign contract for prototype satellite to gather Arctic weather data. *UN-SPIDER News*. https://www.un-spider.org/index.php/news-and-events/news/esa-and-ohb-sweden-sign-contract-prototype-satellite-gather-arctic-weather-data.
34. Wilson Center (2018, June 11). Space Technology for a Smart and Resilient Arctic. Overview. *Wilson Centre – Past*

Events. https://www.wilsoncenter.org/event/space-technology-for-smart-and-resilient-arctic.
35. WIPO [World Intellectual Property Organization] (2011, April 13). *Transfer of Technology. Standing Committee on the Law of Patents,* SCP/14/4 REV. http://www.wipo.int/edocs/mdocs/scp/en/scp_16/scp_14_4_rev.pdf.
36. WTO [World Trade Organization] (1994). Text of Article XVIII, relevant interpretative notes and understanding on the balance-of-payments provisions of GATT 1994. In WTO, *Analytical Index of the GATT* (pp. 488-513). World Trade Organization. https://www.wto.org/english/res_e/publications_e/ai17_e/gatt1994_art18_gatt47.pdf.
37. WTO (2001, November 14). *Doha Ministerial Declaration*, WT/MIN(01)/DEC/1. https://www.wto.org/english/thewto_e/minist_e/min01_e/mindecl_e.htm#technology.
38. WTO, Council for Trade in Goods (2002, January 16). Notification under Section C of Article XVIII of the General Agreement on Tariffs and Trade 1994 and the Decision of 28 November 1979 on Safeguard Action for Development Purposes. Bangladesh, G/C/7.
39. WTO (2019, November 2019). *Natural Disasters and Trade. Study I. Executive Summary.* https://www.wto.org/english/tratop_e/devel_e/study1_exec_summary_sympnaturaldisaster29112019_e.pdf.
40. WTO (2020). *Research on natural disasters and trade.* https://www.wto.org/english/tratop_e/devel_e/a4t_e/researchnaturdisaster_e.htm.
41. Zannoni, D. (2021). Space Law (2019). *Yearbook of International Disaster Law,* 2(1), 529–537. https://doi.org/10.1163/26662531_00201_033.

SPACE OPERATIONS AND THE NATURAL ENVIRONMENT OF THE ARCTIC

Stefan Kirchner & Alvaro Sanabria-Rangel

Abstract: The natural environment of the Arctic and the people who live in the circumpolar global north are increasingly facing pressures. Even activities which are conducted far away can have negative impacts on Arctic communities and the environment on which they depend. Space activities provide services which are mainstays of modern life, such as navigation, weather forecasting and telecommunication. Launches of spacecraft, however, can have negative impacts on the natural environment. This also affects the Arctic. There, environmental pollution affects not only the right to a healthy environment but also the land rights and food security of indigenous peoples. In the last decades, public international law has undergone - and continues to experience - a process of fragmentation, caused by the increasing complexity of international law and its increasing regulatory scope. This fragmentation, even when embedded in quasi-constitutional processes within public international law in general and some fields in particular, creates a risk of legal actors overlooking connections. In the last years, environmental aspects have received some attention from international space lawyers. By emphasizing the human rights dimension of environmental protection, taking into account especially the case law of the European Court of Human Rights, this text aims to show that interconnectedness between fragments of public international law is essential and that human rights concerns can provide the factor which connects the different fragments of public international law. It will be argued that by honoring their existing duty to respect international human rights law states can expand space law without a need for formal changes to the texts of space law treaties, although future space law treaties can, and should, include environmental and human rights obligations *expressis verbis*.

Keywords: Space, satellites, environment, indigenous rights, human rights, Arctic

Introduction

Modern life depends on space operations to a great degree. Space activities have become so commonplace that it is easy to forget just how much we depend on space-related services, in particular on satellites. Satellite broadcasting may be the most obvious example due to the visibility of receiver antennas, but satellites also provide services such as individual telecommunication, weather forecasts and navigation. International law regulates space activities, including the launching and operation of satellites. Space operations create pollution. One of the most obvious examples for pollution created by space activities is space debris, an issue which space law is already beginning to address. But while the geographical focus of international space law is outer space, space operations also have effects on Earth. Today, these effects on both people and the natural environment on Earth are seen also as issues which international law needs to address. In this text it will be shown how international law can be used to tackle these challenges.

The focus of this text is the situation in the Arctic. Europe's primary spaceport is located in Kourou in French Guiana (Hobe, 2019, p. 11), which is part of France and of the European Union, but rockets are also launched from a number of other places across, including the high north. While launch sites near the equator, such as Kourou, are preferable in terms of the energy needed to get the rocket's mass into orbit, northern Europe houses several launch sites, including several locations north of the Arctic Circle, for example the Andøya Space Center in Andenes, Norway, which also operates a second launch site, the Svalbard Rocket Range (SvalRak) in Ny-Ålesund on Svalbard, and Esrange near Kiruna, Sweden. A few hundred kilometers further south, but still relatively far north, at least when compared to other launch sites, Russia's Plesetsk Cosmodrome in Arkhangelsk oblast is located at 62°55'32'' Northern latitude.

Negative Environmental Impacts of Space Operations

Getting satellites into orbit has long become a business, although it is still only one part of space business. Rocket launches are necessary for a range of purposes beyond the deployment of satellites into orbit, for example resupply missions to the International Space Stations (ISS), crewed space flights and research, not only in deep space but also near Earth. Launches from the High North often serve the latter purpose. While reusability is becoming the new norm in launch operations, many launches are still conducted using single-use rocket stages which fall back to Earth. Often, these rockets or rocket stages are too large to burn up completely when reentering the atmosphere. In order to reduce risk to humans, planned reentries are undertaken usually in very remote regions, for example in the so-called "South Pacific Ocean Uninhabited Area" (Davies, 2016) near Point Nemo in the South Pacific. Point Nemo is the "oceanic pole of inaccessibility" (Davies, 2016): About 2,700 km from the nearest (still very remote) islands in the Pacific, Point Nemo is as far from land as one can get at sea (Davies, 2016). In fact, it is said that sometimes the nearest humans are the astronauts and cosmonauts who orbit Earth on board the ISS (Davies, 2016). The choice of this region as the last resting place of spacecraft is aimed at reducing the risk of human casualties, at some risk for the natural environment, albeit in a region where there is little marine life to begin with and which is of very limited economic or other importance for humans.

But the example set by this practice means that the natural environment is seen as expendable for the purposes of rocket and rocket stage return. This has significant and unfortunate implications elsewhere because other locations chosen for the return of rockets or rocket stages are not as far from human habitation. In fact, some of them are of crucial importance for the people who live in remote regions, including the Arctic. The risk of damages to the natural environment and to human health as a result of returning rockets and rocket stages (see in general Kerrest & Thro, 2019) in the Arctic is very real.

Today, indigenous land rights are under pressure from many sides. In particular in the Arctic, the combination of climate change, increasing accessibility of parts of the Arctic (although melting permafrost makes many parts of the Arctic less accessible than before), an increasing demand for natural resources and infrastructure, for example for transport or tourism, contributes to land use conflicts. Under international law, under binding treaties such as the International Labour Organization (ILO) Indigenous and Tribal Peoples Convention of 1989 (ILO, 1989), commonly referred to as ILO Convention 169 or under soft law norms which reflect and develop customary international law, especially the 2007 United Nations Declaration on the Rights of Indigenous Peoples (United Nations, 2007), indigenous peoples enjoy the right to free, prior and informed consent (FPIC), which is a consultation rather than a veto power (cf. Heinämäki & Kirchner, 2017, p. 238). All too often, though, this right is realized only imperfectly, for example in the context of extractive industries (Kirchner, 2018). When it comes to cross-border effects, the Nordic region has been leading in the development of legal options to exchange environmental information across borders and to conduct cross-border environmental impact assessments (EIAs). In particular the latter could be a potent tool for the protection of the rights of local residents, including indigenous communities, who might be affected by rocket launches. To be truly effective, though, such cross-border environmental impact assessments would have to involve all potential actors.

The need to involve all relevant actors in attempts to prevent harm befalling Arctic communities quickly leads to practical difficulties, as the Arctic is small in geographical terms. To put the situation in perspective: the surface area north of the Arctic circle, including both the Arctic Ocean and the surrounding land areas, is roughly 20,000,000 km^2 in size (cf. Marsh & Kaufman, 2013, p. 25), which is just slightly larger than the combined land area of the United States of America and Canada. More than two-thirds of this area, over 14,000,000km^2, consists of the Arctic Ocean. While the political distances between different Arctic states range from almost nil (between the Nordic states) to very serious (between Russia and the West).

Rocket stages launched from northern Russia have come down in Baffin Bay between Greenland and Canada, right in the heart of Inuit

Nunagat, the homeland of the Inuit people which reaches from Greenland (Kalaallit Nunaat) across the northern reaches of Canada (from East to West: Nunatsiavut in the Labrador region of the province of Newfoundland and Labrador, Nunavik in the province of Quebec, the autonomous territory of Nunavut and the Inuvialuit Settlement Region which includes parts of the Northwest Territories and the Yukon Territory) and Alaska all the way to the extreme North-East of the Russian Federation. Other rockets will come down closer to the launch site, either as planned returns or as a result of technical failures, a risk which is very real for the Sámi people as Esrange is in their homeland, Sápmi.

In recent years, the legal community has become more aware of these issues, in no small part due to the 2017 article by *Byers* and *Byers*, entitled "Toxic splash: Russian rocket stages dropped in Arctic waters raise health, environmental and legal concerns" (Byers & Byers, 2017), in which they highlighted the environmental damage caused by leftover rocket fuel from rocket stages which fall into the Northwater Polynya, Pikialasorsuaq, in Baffin Bay. Pikialasorsuaq is the Arctic's largest permanently ice-free area in areas usually covered by sea-ice (Byers & Byers, 2017, p. 582). As such, it provides a unique natural environment and is of great importance to the Inuit people, not only in terms of ensuring their food security through hunting but also in cultural terms.

Also efforts by private and public actors, as well as space-faring efforts by academic institutions in different arctic nations, while providing valuable technical developments and opportunities for the Arctic, can lead to new environmental challenges, especially if launches are conducted in or near the Arctic.

In the European High North, the increasing importance of the Esrange space port on the Swedish side of Sápmi, is giving rise to concerns about the rights of the Sámi people and the protection of the natural environment in the region. Unlike the waters off the Atlantic near Cape Canaveral, Sápmi is not an area devoid of people. To the contrary, it has been home to the Sámi people for thousands of years and today millions of people from different countries and cultural backgrounds call Sápmi their home. Although the region near Esrange is relatively thinly populated, it is not an empty space. Especially in the Arctic, and even more so for indigenous peoples, the integrity of the natural environment is of crucial importance for well-being, sustainable development and the protection of human health. Unlike in large urban settings, there is still a close relationship between humans and nature. In the Arctic, all residents depend on nature. This is even more so for indigenous communities in remote regions, where hunting is an essential aspect of life and survival in the north, not least due to the high prices of food which has to be brought there over large distances. The marine environment in Pikilasorsuaq or the vegetation in Sápmi are important for the animals which are big parts of the respective cultures of the Inuit and Sámi people and important for their food security.

Expanding Space Law
Current public international law, for example the Outer Space Treaty (OST, 1967) and the Liability Convention (LC, 1972), establishes obligations for launch states (OST, 1967: Article VII; LC, 1972). Today, it is recognized that the totality of norms which govern space operations go beyond space law in the narrow sense of the term but also cover environmental concerns (Viikari, 2017). Such environmental considerations are receiving more attention recently, be it in terms of limiting space debris or (Viikari, 2017: 719 et seq.; Stubbe, 2018), as relevant for the topic under discussion here, environmental aspects on Earth (Viikari, 2017, p. 724). Today, reusable rocket stages are gaining a lot of attention. The reason why they are an important development is that for the longest time of spaceflight, rockets were single-use items. Often, this is still the case. Reusability is not just a demand from an environmental perspective but also good business. It is not surprising that private companies rely on reusable transport systems. Just like the possibility to make deorbiting systems for satellites legally obligatory under national space legislations in order to reduce the amount of space debris, which threatens the future of spaceflight from Earth (Stubbe, 2018, p. 223), it is legally

possible that reusability of commercial rocket stages will be legally required in the future. Already today, reusability is a key factor in making space flight sustainable and commercially profitable.

Infusing Indigenous and Environmental Human Rights into Space Law
In the next step it is necessary to remember that international law does not only protect the natural environment *per se* but also for the purpose of protecting human interests. Indigenous land rights also cover marine spaces (Allen et al., 2019) and the rights of the Inuit and Sámi peoples mentioned earlier, or of other indigenous peoples, be it in French Guiana, Sápmi, Greenland, Canada, Russia or elsewhere, have to be respected also in the context of rocket launches.
Among the human rights which have to be respected also by states involved in space operations, such as launches, is the right to a healthy environment. This right has been recognized by a number of courts, most notably by the European Court of Human Rights (ECtHR). Within the framework of the right to private life under Article 8 of the European Convention on Human Rights (ECHR) (Council of Europe, 1950), the ECtHR has recognized the right to a healthy environment, which obliges states which are parties to the ECHR to refrain from activities which harm the natural environment to a degree which endangers human health (McGinley and Egan v. The United Kingdom, 1998, p. 101). This confirmation of the ECtHR's established understanding of the ECHR as a "living instrument" (Tyrer v. UK, 1978, p. 31) infused health concerns into the application of the European Convention on Human Rights, which is more focused on civil and political rights than on economic, social and cultural rights and which does not contain a right to health *expressis verbis*.
The right to a healthy environment has been recognized under both regional human rights systems applicable in the Arctic, the Inter-American human rights system, which includes Canada and the United States, and the system established under the ECHR, to which

Denmark (also with respect to Greenland and Føroyar), Iceland, Norway, Sweden, Finland and the Russian Federation are parties.

The evolving nature of the right to a healthy environment affects our understanding of the relation this right foresees to protect between the individuals or the community as a whole and their local environment. Similarly, the scope of the right to a healthy environment is the basis for a limitation to the action of the states and to private parties when they have consequences to the well-being of a local environment. Roman law set an early precedent in this area of law with an incipient definition of the right to live in a healthy environment. Namely, Roman Law distinguished some types of elements (the air, the water, the sea) that could not be subject to private property. They were considered to be *res communis omnium,* which means that their access could not be restricted (Terrazas Ponce, 2012, p. 132). Accordingly, this early definition of environmental rights (that sees natural resources as unlimited) sets few limitations to the exploitation of natural resources, a definition which differs from the current consensus in this matter. For instance, environmental rights are often linked to the concept of sustainable development which is included in the Interamerican Democratic Charter (Organization of American States, 2001) among other international instruments. The need for sustainability is an acknowledgment that state's policies should take into consideration the impact they may have to the environment and the living conditions of the future generations as well. Therefore, sustainable development could be seen as a burden for the state to harmonize the need for economic growth with the obligation to protect the environment.

In this order of ideas, legal developments on human rights instruments could constraint the ability of human rights courts to interpret the scope of the right to live in a healthy environment. In the case of the European Court of Human Rights and the Inter-American Court of Human Rights, it is observed that the latter has benefitted from a more prolific definition of the right to a healthy environment by the relevant human rights instruments. Namely, Article 11 of the Protocol of San Salvador to the American Convention on Human Rights

(Organization of American States, 1988), in the Inter-American system of human rights, introduces the right to a healthy environment as a separate right in this system. On the other hand, in the European System of Human Rights protection there is not an equivalent to the Protocol of San Salvador. To this date a Protocol to the European Convention on Human Rights has not been adopted that includes the right to a healthy environment as a separate right.

However, these circumstances do not mean that the right to a healthy environment is inexistent as it is indeed a natural development of the fundamental rights which are codified in the European Convention on Human Rights. The lack of a more detailed codification to this right rather responds to the circumstances surrounding the adoption of the European Convention on Human Rights in 1950 in a post-World War II Europe. Conversely, Article 37 of the 2000 European Charter of Fundamental Rights (European Convention, 2000) is a more recent example at the European Union level of a consensus among European governments on the need to codify and strengthen the enforceability of this right. In this order of ideas, the lack of a specific article linked to the right to live in a healthy environment has not barred the European Court of Human Rights to judge whether this right has been violated or not. However, the lack of a more specific provision has had an impact on the outcome of the cases studied by the European Court of Human Rights as it will be examined below.

The right to a healthy environment can be read as a manifestation of the right to life (Article 2 ECHR). There are both legal and scientific reasons to argue that the right to life cannot be isolated and understood as the bare minimum biological conditions for human life to remain viable. From a scientific perspective, even if it is appealed to an extreme scenario, a number of conditions have to be met to make human life possible. These conditions depend on the surrounding environment. For instance, in order to protect the right to life, there must be certain conditions such as access to water, food and healthy conditions. Additionally, in order to fully protect the right to life it is necessary to read this right together with other human rights guiding principles such as human dignity. The Inter-American Court of Human Rights has expressed that the concept of a dignified living conditions (*vida digna*) is closely related to the concept of vulnerability. Due to the fundamental nature of the right to life a restrictive approach to this concept would be inadmissible. Every human has in addition to the right to not be deprived of his life arbitrarily, the right that he will not be prevented from having access to the conditions that guarantee a dignified existence (Villagran-Morales et al. v. Guatemala, 1999, p. 144). Similarly, the European Court of Human Rights has stated that human dignity is a guiding principle along with the right to human freedom that is part of the very essence of the European Convention on Human Rights (Christine Goodwin v. UK, 2002, p. 90). Furthermore, the European Court of Human Rights took into consideration the concept of dignity in relation to the right to privacy and family life protected in Article 8 of the European Convention on Human Rights. Human dignity plays a role when the scope of this and any other right under the conventions are discussed. In this case, the notion of quality of life had a significant importance (Pretty v. UK, 2002, p. 65). Therefore, a number of certain prerequisites should be fulfilled so people's right to life is protected in decent and safe conditions. These prerequisites are part of the right to a healthy environment (Cançado Trindade, 1993, pp. 15-45).

Following this line of reasoning, the right to a healthy environment is recognized in the European system of Human Rights as a consequence of its inherent relationship with the rights to life (Article 2 ECHR), possessions (Article 1, protocol 1), fair trial (Article 6 ECHR) and in some cases, freedom of expression (Article 10 ECHR) of the European Convention on Human Rights. Notwithstanding the latter statement, the absence of a more concise source pointing out to this right in the European Convention has set a limitation to the possibility of finding a violation to the right to live in a healthy environment. This was the case in *Kyrtatos v. Greece*. The European Court of Human Rights concluded in this case that for the Court to study a case concerning environmental pollution, there had to be a direct connection between the environmental damage and a violation to the right to private and family life (Kyrtatos v. Greece, 2003, p. 52). The European Court of Human Rights found, for the first time, a link between the right to a private and family life and the environmental effects caused to the victim by the industrial activities of a plant for the treatment of liquid and solid waste in *López Ostra v. Spain*. In this case, the European Court of Human Rights ruled out that the consequences of the project had put the claimant, her family and the whole neighborhood where she lived in a situation that affected her private and family life and put their health at risk. This violation was caused by a change in the environmental factors caused by the project. Hence, the Court was open to recognize the right to live in a healthy environment, although its recognition is limited to proofing a connection with other rights explicitly recognized in the European Convention on Human Rights.

In the *Taşkin and others v. Turkey* decision, the European Court of Human Rights sided with the Supreme Administrative Court of Turkey in a case related to a permission granted by the Turkish government to extract gold in a mine. The Supreme Administrative Court of Turkey initially concluded that a permit issued by the government to extract gold in the Ovacik mine should have been annulled. The reason was that because of the location of the mine, the mining process would have had a negative impact to the ecosystem and to human life. The Supreme Administrative Court found a violation to the right to life and to a healthy environment of the inhabitants. The European Court of Human Rights on its part considered that the government did not give enough consideration to this judicial decision. This omission of the potential impact of a project on the environment of the locals constituted on itself a violation to the right to private and family life (Taşkin and others v. Turkey, 2004, pp. 118-125).

In the current case of study, the aforementioned cases decided by the European Court of Human Rights can offer us some light on how environmental damages in indigenous-used lands in the Arctic by activities such as the launching of space rockets trigger a violation to the European Convention of Human Rights. Firstly, according to the decision in *Kyrtatos v. Greece* there must be a disruption to the right to private and family life caused by space activities in the Arctic. In the case of *Kyrtatos v. Greece,* there was a deterioration of the environment. However, this damage in the proximity of the applicant's property did not directly affect his own wellbeing. Secondly, a case like *López Ostra v. Spain* illustrates how the change in environmental factors caused by a project may lead to a violation to the right to private and family life. Notwithstanding the potential benefits that space activities may have, there should be enough consideration to the adverse effects in the environment these activities may have. Finally, *Taşkin and others v. Turkey* puts a burden on the state in which space activities such as the launching of rockets will take place. The issue of a permit to perform these activities should consider the chosen location and the potential impact to human life and the ecosystem in this area.

The right to a healthy environment is not limited to the European human rights system. Importantly, it has also been recognized, albeit in a somewhat different form, in the inter-american system of international human rights protection (Organization of American States, 1969). In the following paragraphs, we will take a short look at the case law in the Inter-American system to show that alternative approaches to environmental human rights are possible. While many of the cases dealt with in the Inter-American human rights system might seem geographically far from the Arctic, the impact of the Inter-American Court of Human Rights on the development of global human rights standards, in particular in the context of indigenous rights, is not to be underestimated.

The Protocol of San Salvador to the Inter-American Convention on Human Rights (Organization of American States, 1988) which focused on economic, social and cultural rights includes in Article 11 the right to a healthy environment which encompasses an obligation for the states to promote the protection, preservation and improvement of the environment. The Inter-American Court of Human Rights considered the right to a healthy environment as both an individual and collective right. In an advisory opinion, the Court said that a violation to this right affects particularly vulnerable groups

(Inter-American Court of Human Rights, 2017, pp. 59, 67). Both individuals or groups under a circumstance that puts them in a situation of vulnerability are struck with more intensity by a change to their local environments. For instance, in the case of indigenous groups whose traditional form of living are linked to their lands, their survival as a group could be endangered by a project that may change the usage of their lands (Kaliña and Lokoño v. Surinam, 2015, pp. 199-203). In a similar fashion, economically disadvantaged groups would be impacted with more intensity if they were forced to move to a different place or to endure the negative impact that a project in their proximity may have on their health (Saramaka People v. Suriname, 2007, pp. 129-132; Indigenous Communities of the Lhaka Honhat (our land association) v. Argentina, 2020, pp. 272-289).

The Inter-American Court of Human Rights has studied in particular the cases of indigenous peoples in situations in which projects taking part in their territories affect their local environments. In these situations, the Court has taken into consideration the situation of these groups and the connection between their traditional forms of living and their lands as well as how these traditions could be endangered. In the case of the *Yakye Axa Indigenous Community v. Paraguay,* the Inter-American Court of Human Rights found that this community was in a state of extreme poverty affecting their access to safe water, food, health and housing (Yakye Axa Indigenous Community v. Paraguay, 2005, pp. 163-167). This situation was caused because they had lost access to their ancestral territories. In this case the Inter-American Court found a violation to the right to live in a healthy environment in connection with a violation to the right of life with dignity (Article 1 of the American Convention), the right to health, food, education and to the benefits of culture (Articles 10, 12, 13, 14 of the San Salvador Protocol). It also found that ILO Convention No. 169 on Indigenous and Tribal Peoples (International Labour Organization, 1989) had been violated (Yakye Axa Indigenous Community v.Paraguay, 2005, p. 163).

Moreover, the right to private property contained in Article 21 of the American Convention has been used as a source to protect the right to live in a healthy environment in the jurisprudence of the Inter-American Court of Human Rights. The Inter-American Court of Human Rights has understood that, in the case of indigenous and tribal peoples the concept of private property is broadly defined and it includes the natural resources in the territory of the community. The right to property of indigenous groups can be limited as in other cases related to private property. However, the Inter-American Court considered that in these cases there is an additional requirement to the general test it applies in the case of a human right limitation. Accordingly, it is necessary to verify that a limitation to the right to collective property of indigenous groups does not deny their subsistence as a people (Saramaka People v. Suriname, 2007, pp. 128-129). The right to property is closely connected to the question of land ownership and usage rights, which in turn is elementary for the exercise of the traditional livelihoods by indigenous peoples.

The right to live in a healthy environment, as a human right, requires to assess in some cases whether the state fulfills its obligation to prevent any violation to this right. In the Inter-American System of Human Rights, Article 1.1 of the American Convention on Human Rights is the legal basis for this minimum threshold. Article 1.1 of the American Convention contains a general obligation to prevent, investigate and redress any human rights violation. In order to answer this question, it is necessary to examine whether a state has taken effective measures to protect this right. Therefore, the first step Courts could take to answer this question is to examine the domestic legislation enacted at the time by the state and evaluate whether there are effective, available mechanisms to enforce the right (Inter-American Court of Human Rights, 1993, pp. 26-27).

The obligation to prevent a violation to the right to live in a healthy environment is closely related to the same obligation for the right to life as it was stated above. In this respect, the Inter-American Court of Human Rights has stated that states should take all appropriate measures to protect and preserve the lives of everyone under its jurisdiction (Pueblo Bello Massacre v. Colombia, 2006:120). In this order of ideas, states have the burden of proof that they have adopted concrete measures to protect the rights of the plaintiffs and that these measures were appropriate in the concrete case to protect and preserve the right to life. This requirement is especially significant in the cases of victims from vulnerable groups (Yakye Axa Indigenous Community v.Paraguay, 2005, pp. 162).

The Inter-American Court of Human Rights referred more specifically to the obligation to prevent a violation in the context of the right to live in a healthy environment on its Advisory Opinion OC 23/17. Notwithstanding that it is not an exhaustive definition of what this obligation entails, the Court asserted that significant damages to the environment must be prevented. This means that states have an active role implementing regulations, monitoring and supervising the activities that could have a negative impact to the environment. By the same token, when damage to the environment has been produced all necessary actions to mitigate the damages should be taken (Inter-American Court of Human Rights, 2017, p. 127). The precautionary principle is suggested by the Inter-American Court as an indicator to measure whether the actions taken have been protective enough of the right to live in a healthy environment or not. According to the precautionary principle, when there is evidence that a certain activity may cause a serious and irreversible damage to the environment, states should adopt protective measures and act accordingly. The lack of scientific certainty over the environmental consequences of an activity should not be used as an excuse in order not to act with precaution (Inter-American Court of Human Rights, 2017, p. 180).

The European Court of Human Rights has also assessed whether a state has taken sufficient precautionary measures in a project that has an impact on the environment. In *Tătar vs. Romania*, the Court found a violation to the right to private life (Tătar vs. Romania, 2009, pp. 121-125). To do so, the Court took into account the inaction of the state in a situation in which there was a serious and substantial risk to the health and wellbeing of the plaintiffs (Tătar vs. Romania, 2009, pp. 98-125). In this case, the European Court of Human Rights examined the evidence pointing to a risk to the environment and public health caused by gold extraction activities using cyanide-based technology. In order to protect the right to private life, the state had the obligation to take all reasonable measures to protect this right including the right to enjoy a healthy environment. In this case, the state failed to properly consider the available evidence including a scientific study on the risks of the mining activities to take place, when it authorized a company to start its extracting activities (Tătar vs. Romania, 2009, pp. 89-97).

In their jurisprudence both the European Court of Human Rights and the Inter-American Court of Human Rights have recognized the need to protect the right to live in a healthy environment. In the case of the Inter-American Court of Human Rights, Article 11 of the San Salvador Protocol has allowed it to assess this right separately as well as in connection with other rights, in particular the right to life in dignity. Dignity as a legal concept has an important role to play also in the defense of the rights of indigenous peoples (Kirchner & Koivurova, 2020). The European Court of Human Rights has also considered the violation of the right to private and family life caused by environmental damages. The lack of a specific provision on the right to live in a healthy environment is not an insurmountable obstacle to further develop its jurisprudence on the right to live in a healthy environment. As a living instrument, there is room to further develop the European Convention on Human Rights in this area of law. For instance, the European Court of Human Rights could examine in the future Article 1 of Protocol 1 to the European Convention on Human Rights to assess the collective right of the inhabitants of a place to enjoy the environment as a property right. The duty to protect the right to a healthy environment obligation extends to regulation of acts by private actors - including issuing permits for rocket launches. When considering permits for space launches, these considerations need to be taken into account already under the *lex lata*, at least in states which are parties to the ECHR and the ACHR.

Fragmentation and Constitutionalisation of Public International Law

These legal considerations for space operations from outside classical space law, however, need to be seen also in a wider context, taking into account the development of public international law in general. Two trends, which have been observed since the 1980s, remain relevant in this regard.

International law is becoming more and more complex and different parts of international law are more and more seen as standing apart from each other. Due to the increasing complexity of public international law, it is also becoming more and more difficult for international lawyers to grasp the entirety of public international law. Specialization is a necessary reaction of our profession to the increasing complexity. For centuries, the sets of rules which we consider to make up public international law have been splitting into multiple subsets of rules: the law of the sea, the laws of war, regulations concerning diplomatic and consular relations, human rights law, space law etc. Specialization has become a practical necessity. There is a risk in this inevitable fragmentation and specialization, namely the risk that connections are overlooked and that public international law becomes too removed from the practical reality of the people whom every law is meant to serve. If we truly understand law, including public international law, to be in the service of human society, it cannot be merely imposed but has to react to specific needs. Public international law has long had a very reactive nature. Today, the community of international lawyers (on this specific community see already Schachter, 1977/78) is called upon to develop international law further, in the service of humankind as a whole.

As awareness of the connection between human rights and the environment grows and environmental human rights are entering the mainstream of legal and political discourses, space law is evolving beyond its traditional definitions. Modern space law is not limited to space law treaties and related regulatory efforts but today also has an environmental dimension. As public international law becomes the realm of specialists, it is incumbent on the community of international lawyers not to lose sight of the greater picture. Protecting human rights (Baehr & Castermanns-Holleman, 2004, p. 2) and the natural environment are tasks for the international community as a whole. Parallel to the fragmentation of international law, public international law has also undergone a process of constitutionalization. Today, the protection of human rights can be seen as a quasi-constitutional duty under public international law (cf. Kirchner, 2004, p. 59). Although the Charter of the United Nations (United Nations, 1945) which, after all, was adopted already more than 75 years ago, remains silent on environmental issues, the United Nations Security Council, has taken environmental issues into account in its deliberations on numerous occasions, although it has not yet deemed environmental pollution or degradation, nor climate change, as a threat to peace within the meaning of Article 39 UN Charter. Given the increasing redefinition of security and the relevance of the natural environment for human security, it does become conceivable that, were the political conditions supportive, the UN Security council might follow its own precedent regarding the right to democracy (cf. Shaw, 2017, p. 949) and elevate environmental concerns to this quasi-constitutional level of public international law as well. Sustainability and circular economy principles are becoming more enshrined in legal norms and technical rules created on the international level can contribute to making space operations greener and more sustainable. The space law community would be well advised to take into account the regulatory systems already existing within the frameworks of the International Maritime Organization (IMO) and the International Civil Aviation Organization (ICAO). These legal frameworks allow for the creation of specialized legal norms, which benefit from the technical expertise of people working in the respective fields. These technical norms are created within the frameworks provided for by international treaties. An important example is the Polar Code, a binding set of norms on ship operations in Arctic waters and in the Southern Ocean, which entered into force in 2017 and which is binding due to its legal basis in the International

Convention for the Safety of Life at Sea (SOLAS) and the International Convention for the Prevention of Pollution from Ships (MARPOL). Already today, the United Nations Office on Outer Space Affairs (UNOOSA) is actively advocating space sustainability.

This future-oriented approach should be shared by nation states. Subjects of international law, in particular states, but also international lawyers, both in practice and in academia, no longer have the luxury to focus only on the question of what the law is today. Practising attorneys who want to advise their clients also have to be aware of trends and future developments. While a decision in an individual case requires the look back at the law as it was at the time in question, a concept also enshrined in public international law in the form of the principle of intertemporal international law (Dörr, 2018, p. 655; Elias, 1980), a holistic approach to the legal profession also requires a forward looking approach, anticipating future developments. Just as lawyers have to be cognizant of emerging trends, states have to take technical trends and their potential impact on humans, in particular those within their jurisdictions, when contributing to the development of public international law in general and space law in particular. In the context of the jurisprudence of the European Court of Human Rights regarding the meaning of the term "jurisdiction" in Article 1 of the European Convention on Human Rights, governments of states which are parties to the ECHR are well advised to remember that the term "jurisdiction" is very broad and that under specific circumstances states can also be held legally responsible for violations of human rights which take effect beyond their own borders as the interaction between the state and the affected person can establish a bond which amounts to jurisdiction within the meaning of Article 1 ECHR.

Concluding Remarks
Beyond specific obligations, the evolution of international human rights law in recent decades and its pervasiveness across legal orders highlights the fact that specific values (cf. Kirchner, 2004) have been

given the power of law through international human rights law. Today, international human rights law can be seen as a quasi-constitutional bracket which surrounds the fragments of public international law. It can therefore be argued that by honoring their existing duty to respect international human rights law states can expand space law without a need for formal changes to the texts of space law treaties, although future space law treaties can, and should, include environmental and human rights obligations *expressis verbis*.

Especially for lawyers who are working in rather technical areas of public international law, like space law, this means that it is necessary to look beyond the formal limitations of our respective disciplines. Today, space law can no longer be seen as disconnected from environmental law or human rights. This is not an entirely new trend. In the last decade, there has been an increasing awareness of the importance of human rights in the maritime sector. Space law has long been inspired by the law of the sea, just like we still use many naval references in a space context. We speak of space *ships* and astro-, cosmo- and taiko*nauts*, like ships, spaceships are required to be registered. There must be a connection between a ship and its flag state (United Nations, 1992, p. 91). Similarly, spacecraft have to be registered in registries organized by nation states (United Nations, 1974, p. 2), the obligation to provide assistance in emergencies is enshrined in international law etc. Trends seen in the maritime sector, such as a stronger focus on the protection of the environment and of human rights, are already becoming considerations for the space industry as well. It seems reasonable to assume that such values will also be given the shape and force of international law and domestic regulations.

In addition to organizational rules, for example the law of treaties or the law of state responsibility, human rights form a kind of quasi-constitutional dimension of public international law. If they were to be taken up, for example in resolutions by the United Nations Security Council, environmental and climate change aspects could be elevated to the same level, not only as part of international human rights law but as quasi-constitutional international legal considerations *per se*. Already today, international human rights law provides the bracket which connects the fragments which make up contemporary international law. While it can be tempting in an ever more complex world to seek intellectual refuge in a small field of expertise, the application of international law requires an understanding of the practical realities to which the law is applied, including emerging and future challenges. It would therefore behoove the space law community to broaden its view beyond the sets of norms which are usually considered to make up international space law in a formal sense and to take into account also indigenous rights and environmental human rights aspects.

References
1. Allen, Stephen, Nigel Bankes & Øyvind Ravna (eds.) (2019). The Rights of Indigenous Peoples in Maritime Areas. Portland: Hart Publishing.
2. American Convention on Human Rights, 1969, Organization of American States
3. Baehr, Peter R. & Monique Castermans-Holleman (2004). The Role of Human Rights in Foreign Policy. London: Palgrave Macmillan.
4. Byers, Michael & Byers, Cameron (2017). "Toxic splash: Russian rocket stages dropped in Arctic waters raise health, environmental and legal concerns", 53 Polar Record, pp. 580-591, https://doi.org/10.1017/S0032247417000547.
5. Cançado Trindade, Antônio Augusto (1993), Environment and Development: Formulation and Implementation of the Right to Development as a Human Right, pp. 15-45, In: Asian Yearbook of International Law, Volume 3, Kluwer Academic Publishers.
6. Churchill, R. R. & Lowe, A. V. (1999). The law of the sea. Manchester: Manchester University Press.
7. Council of Europe (1950). Convention for the Protection of Human Rights and Fundamental Freedoms [European Convention on Human Rights], European Treaty Series No. 5.
8. Council of Europe (1952). Protocol to the Convention for the Protection of Human Rights and Fundamental Freedoms
9. Davies, Ella (2016). "The place furthest from land is known as Point Nemo", *BBC*, 5 October 2016, http://www.bbc.com/earth/story/20161004-the-place-furthest-from-land-is-known-as-point-nemo.
10. Dörr, Oliver (2018). "7. Kapitel: Völkerrechtliche Verantwortlichkeit", in: Volker Epping & Wolff Heintschel von Heinegg (eds.), Völkerrecht. Munich: C. H. Beck, pp. 625-691.

11. Elias, T. O. (1980). "The Doctrine of Intertemporal Law", 74 American Journal of International Law 285-307, https://doi.org/10.2307/2201503.
12. European Court of Human Rights, Christine Goodwin v. UK Judgment, July 11, 2002.
13. European Court of Human Rights, Kyrtatos v. Greece Judgment, August 22, 2003.
14. European Court of Human Rights, Pretty v. UK Judgment, April 29, 2002.
15. European Court of Human Rights, Taşkin and others v. Turkey Judgment, November 10, 2004.
16. European Court of Human Rights, Tătar vs. Romania Judgment, January 27, 2009.
17. European Court of Human Rights, McGinley and Egan v. The United Kingdom Judgment, June 9, 1998.
18. Heinämäki, Leena & Stefan Kirchner (2017). "Assessment on Recent Developments Regarding Indigenous Peoples' Legal Status and Rights in International Law: with Special Focus on Free, Prior and Informed Consent", in: in: Heinämäki, Leena et al., Saamelaisten oikeuksien toteutuminen: kansainvälinen oikeusvertaileva tutkimus. Helsinki: Valtioneuvoston kanslia, 224-282 (Valtioneuvoston selvitys- ja tutkimustoiminnan julkaisusarja; No. 4, Vol. 2017).
19. Hobe, Stephan (2019). Space Law. Munich: Beck.
20. Hoffmann, Jan Martin Hoffmann, Tüngler, Grit & Kirchner, Stefan (2013). "Europarechtliche Unfallhaftung und Versicherungspflicht der Anbieter von Seereisen", 24 Europäische Zeitschrift für Wirtschaftsrecht / European Journal of Business Law / Revue Européenne de Droit Économique (2013), pp. 332-335.
21. ILO (1989). Indigenous and Tribal Peoples' Convention, ILO Convention No. 169.
22. Inter-American Court of Human Rights, Advisory Opinion OC-13/93, July 16, 1993.

23. Inter-American Court of Human Rights, Advisory Opinion OC-23/17, November 15, 2017.
24. Inter-American Court of Human Rights, Indigenous Communities of the Lhaka Honhat (our land association) v. Argentina, February 06, 2020.
25. Inter-American Court of Human Rights, Kaliña and Lokoño v. Surinam, November 25, 2015
26. Inter-Amereican Court of Human Rights, Pueblo Bello Massacre v. Colombia Judgment January 31, 2006.
27. Inter-American Court of Human Rights, Saramaka People v. Suriname Judgment, November 28, 2007.
28. Inter-American Court of Human Rights, Villagran-Morales et al. v. Guatemala Judgment, November 19, 1999.
29. Yakye Axa Indigenous Community v. Paraguay Judgment, Inter-American Court of Human Rights, June 17, 2005.
30. Inter-American Democratic Charter, 2001
31. Kerrest, Armel & Thro, Caroline (2019). "Liability for damage caused by space activities", in: Jakhu, Ram S. & Dempsey, Paul Stephen (eds.), *Routledge Handbook of Space Law*, Abingdon: Routledge, pp. 59-72.
32. Kirchner, Stefan (2004). "Relative Normativity and the Constitutional Dimension of International Law: A Place for Values in the International Legal System?", 5 German Law Journal, pp. 47-64, https://doi.org/10.1017/S2071832200012244.
33. Kirchner, Stefan (2018). "Indigenous Rights and Livelihoods as Concerns in the Decision-Making on Extractive Industries in Finland", in: Hossain, Kamrul et al. (eds.), Human and Social Security in the Circumpolar Arctic. Leiden: Brill Nijhoff, pp. 263-280.
34. Kirchner, Stefan & Timo Koivurova (2020). "Lawyers' Role in the Protection of Human Dignity of Indigenous Persons", in: Andrea Gattini, Rosana Garciandia, und Philippa Webb (eds.), Human Dignity and International Law. Leiden: Brill Nijhoff, pp. 110-112, https://doi.org/10.1163/9789004435650_011.

35. Kirchner, Stefan, Tüngler, Grit & Hoffmann, Jan Martin (2015). "Carrier Liability for Damages incurred by Ship Passengers: The European Union as a Trailblazer towards a Global Liability Regime?", in: 23 University of Miami International and Comparative Law Review (2015), pp. 193-214.
36. Koivurova, Timo; Kleemola-Juntunen, Pirjo & Kirchner, Stefan (2019). "Emergence of a New Ocean: How to React to the Massive Change?", in: Coats, K. S. & Holroyd, C. (eds.), The Palgrave Handbook of Arctic Policy and Politics. Basingstoke: Palgrave Macmillan, 409-425.
37. LC (1972). Convention on International Liability for Damage Caused by Space Objects [Liability Convention], 961 United Nations Treaty Series 13810.
38. William M. Marsh, William M. & Martin M. Kaufman (2013), Physical Geography - Great Systems and Global Environments, Cambridge: Cambridge University Press.
39. OST (1967). Treaty on Principles Governing the Activities of States in the Exploration and Use of Outer Space, including the Moon and Other Celestial Bodies [Outer Space Treaty], 610 United Nations Treaty Series 8843.
40. Regulation (EC) No. 392/2009 of the European Parliament and of the Council of 23 April 2009 on the liability of carriers of passengers by sea in the event of accidents, Official Journal 2009 L 131/24, https://eur-lex.europa.eu/LexUriServ/LexUriServ.do?uri=OJ:L:2009:131:0024:0046:EN:PDF.
41. Schachter, Oscar (1977/78). "The Invisible College of International Lawyers", 73 Northwestern University Law Review 217-226.
42. Scott, Karen N. & VanderZwaag, David L. (2017). "Polar Oceans and the Law of the Sea", in: Rothwell, Donald R., Oude Elferink, Alex G., Scott, Karen N. & Stephens, Tim (eds)., The Oxford Handbook of the Law of the Sea. Oxford: Oxford University Press, pp. 724-751.

43. Shaw, Malcolm (2017). International Law. Oxford: Oxford University Press.
44. Stubbe, Peter (2018). State Accountability for Space Debris - A Legal Study of Responsibility for Polluting the Space Environment and Liability for Damage caused by Space Debris. Leiden: Brill Nijhoff.
45. Tanaka, Yoshifumi (2019). The International Law of the Sea. Cambridge: Cambridge University Press.
46. Terrazas Ponce, Juan David (2012), El concepto de "res" en los juristas Romanos, II: Las "res communes omnium" [The concept of "res" in the Roman jurists, II: The "res communes omnium"], p. 132, In: Revista de Estudios Histórico-Jurídicos [Sección Derecho Romano] XXXIV (Valparaíso, Chile, 2012).
47. United Nations (1945). Charter of the United Nations, https://www.un.org/en/charter-united-nations/.
48. United Nations (1992), United Nations Convention on the Law of the Sea.
49. United Nations (2007). United Nations Declaration on the Rights of Indigenous Peoples, https://www.un.org/development/desa/indigenouspeoples/wp-content/uploads/sites/19/2018/11/UNDRIP_E_web.pdf.
50. United Nations (1974), Convention on Registration of Objects Launched Into Outer Space.
51. Viikari, Lotta (2017). "Environmental aspects of space activities", in: von der Dunk, Frans & Tronchetti, Fabio (eds.), *Handbook of Space Law*. Cheltenham: Edward Elgar, pp. 717-768.
52. Vizthum, Wolfgang Graf (2006). "Begriff, Geschichte und Rechtsquellen des Seerechts", in: Vizthum, Wolfgang Graf (ed.), Handbuch des Seerechts. Munich: C. H. Beck, pp. 1-61

THE EUROPEAN UNION'S PROPOSAL FOR A BAN ON ARCTIC OIL, GAS AND COAL EXPLOITATION AND TRADE

Stefan Kirchner

On 13 October 2021, the European Commission and the High Representative of the Union for Foreign Affairs and Security Policy presented the EU's updated Arctic policy in the form of a joint communication to the European Parliament, the Council, the European Economic and Social Committee and the Committee of the Regions entitled "A stronger EU engagement for a peaceful, sustainable and prosperous Arctic".

As a detailed analysis of the entire document would exceed the limitations of this format, the focus of this text will be on the one aspect of the EU's 2021 Arctic policy (European Union, 2021) that has attracted a lot of attention. On page 10 of the joint communication, the Commission and the High Representative state that "[b]uilding on the partial moratoriums on hydrocarbons exploration in the Arctic, the EU is committed to ensuring that oil, coal and gas stay in the ground, including in Arctic regions" (European Union, 2021). This statement, which has to be seen in the EU's efforts to combat climate change, such as the European Green Deal and the resilience and recovery efforts in the context of the ongoing COVID-19 pandemic, highlights a commitment to renewable energies.

The new joint communication was not created in a vacuum but is the result of a long learning process in Brussels: the 2008 Arctic policy still saw the hydrocarbons as an opportunity to enhance energy security in the EU (European Union, 2008, section 3.1). In 2011, the EP already placed significantly more emphasis on the sustainable development of the Arctic (European Union, 2011), assuming that hydrocarbon exploitation would continue to happen in the Arctic but arguing for better environmental protections based on "broad all-encompassing ecosystem-based approaches" (European Union, 2011, para. 41). This call for sustainable development was taken up by the

Commission in its Arctic policy document issued in 2012 (European Union 2012, part. 2.2) and by the Council in its 2014 conclusions (European Union, 2014, para. 8). The 2016 policy document (European Union, 2016a), that actually was titled as such, placed a particular emphasis on climate change (European Union, 2016a, part 1) and sustainable development (European Union, 2016a, part 2). The title of the 2021 joint communication echoes the 2016 conclusions by the Council, in which the latter "emphasize[d] the importance of a safe, sustainable and prosperous Arctic" (European Union, 2016, para. 2).

With regard to fossil fuels, however, the new joint communication marks a clear departure from the course of the past, and the impression left by the effects of climate change that are already visible today is undeniable. With this joint communication, the EU has declared the beginning of the end of hydrocarbon extraction, not just in the Arctic but globally. It remains to be seen what the practical impact of this one sentence in a policy document will be and how this will relate into legal obligations on the EU and international levels in the long run. It is important to note that the EU does not intend to create rules unilaterally, by passing legislation on the EU level. Instead, the Commission plans to "work with partners towards a multilateral legal obligation not to allow any further hydrocarbon reserve development in the Arctic or contiguous regions, nor to purchase such hydrocarbons if they were to be produced" (European Union, 2021, p. 10).

This phrase contains two goals: the creation of an internationally binding legal obligation outlawing Arctic hydrocarbon development on one hand and a legally binding obligation to refrain from purchasing such hydrocarbons. The former aspect will require the consent of the Arctic states, most likely in the form of an international treaty. Given the relevance of hydrocarbon extraction for the national economies of Arctic nations such as Russia, Canada or Norway, and the political controversies surrounding Arctic hydrocarbon exploitation in the United States, such a treaty appears elusive at the moment, although the general international legal momentum is away from hydrocarbon extraction. The creation of an international treaty that will actually outlaw the exploration and exploitation of oil, gas and coal in the Arctic will require overcoming not just political obstacles but also the clarification of legal questions, for example the relation between such a hypothetical treaty on one hand and the Svalbard Treaty or the United Nations Convention on the Law of the Sea on the other hand. The use of the terms "exploration" (European Union, 2021, p. 10) and "hydrocarbon reserve development" (European Union, 2021, p. 10) might indicate that this is meant to refer to areas of the Arctic where such exploration has not yet happened and where hydrocarbon exploitation is not yet happening at the moment, although this short passage in the joint communication should not be mistaken for a first draft of a future treaty norm. The aspirational nature of the plan outlined by the Commission is not only visible from the use of the word "shall" (European Union, 2021, p. 10) in this context but also from the unclear geographical scope of this idea, as the text refers to "the Arctic or contiguous regions" (European Union, 2021, p. 10). The joint communication does not provide any clarity what is meant with this phrase (the terminology might be inspired by the subtitle of the academic journal *Arctic Anthropology - an international journal devoted to all aspects of the science of man in the arctic, subarctic and contiguous regions of the world both past and present*). The second tool to contribute to keeping hydrocarbons "in the ground" (European Union, 2021, p. 10) could be utilized immediately if EU states would refrain from purchasing oil and gas from Arctic countries. While this would raise a number of legal issues in terms of trade relations, the right of the peoples of the Arctic to economic self-determination must not be ignored. Accordingly, the EU was well advised to pursue these goals only in cooperation with Arctic partners and based on already existing moratoriums on hydrocarbon exploration that already exist in the North American Arctic, including Greenland (European Union, 2021, p. 10, see also fn. 35). International cooperation remains essential to achieve the goals the EU has outlined in its new joint communication.

It is, however, important to see this passage in the EU's new Arctic strategy in a wider context. As the EU explained in information provided to media on the date of the release of the joint communication, "The call in the new Arctic Strategy for limiting fossil fuel extraction aims to speed up for global energy transition. The EU is committed to implementing the Paris agreement, and oil, coal and gas have the biggest impact on climate change. This is why the EU is pushing for oil, coal and gas to stay in the ground, including in Arctic regions. The International Energy Agency's report on Net Zero by 2050 clearly stated that: "No new oil and natural gas fields are needed in the net zero pathway" (European Union, 2021a). With the explicit call to keep hydrocarbons in the ground, the EU once more makes it clear that it is committed to the transition to an economy that is no longer dependent on burning ancient hydrocarbons. While this might be interpreted by some as a message to Moscow, a more holistic view beyond the current gas crisis is necessary to appropriately evaluate the EU's approach in this matter. In order to limit climate change soon, drastic action is necessary (Lowen, 2021). This includes rethinking policies, their contents and the way they are made.

The Arctic can be seen as testing ground for new forms of international governance, in particular as far as the inclusion of local stakeholders, including indigenous peoples, is concerned. In recent years, the EU has shown an increasing interest in the reality of the people who live in the Arctic, in particular the situation of the indigenous Sámi people. That the European Union is home to seven indigenous peoples, the Sámi in Sweden and Finland, and the six indigenous nations of French Guiana, is often forgotten. While these communities might be small in number and pursuing lifestyles that might be far removed from Berlaymont, it is important to remember that indigenous rights are not only a matter of foreign policy. The new Arctic policy document highlights the desire of the Commission to continue the ongoing dialogue with representatives of the Sámi people. Effectively fighting climate change and protecting the Arctic environment require cooperation, not only between governments but with all concerned stakeholders.

The new policy comes at an important time for the future of the Arctic. At this specific historical moment when the Arctic holds global attention and when climate change is becoming a mainstream concern, while some governments, such as those of China, India, Australia and Germany, still try to hold on to fossil fuels, such as burning coal and lignite for the generation of electric energy, there is a small window of opportunity to end hydrocarbon extraction in the Arctic. Neither Russia nor Norway are likely to join into this effort anytime soon, although the differences between the Arctic neighbors are stark: Norway is decarbonizing its domestic economy while exporting hydrocarbons for the time being, while Russia's current government plans to build the country's economic future on the export of hydrocarbons from the Arctic, at least for the next few decades. The EU's joint communication takes the likelihood of a lack of consensus into account by aiming for the creation of a rule to ban the purchase of Arctic hydrocarbons. At this moment, there might be a possibility to build political momentum in this direction, even if consensus seems elusive. The burning of fossil fuels poses a threat to the natural environment and to the peoples of the Arctic, but the extractive industries, including oil, coal, gas and mining for metals and minerals, create employment for residents in sparsely populated regions where income opportunities are limited. Like elsewhere, the transition to a 'greener' economy in the Arctic also needs to consider the social dimension.

When it comes to the impact of climate change on human communities, the Arctic is the canary in the coal mine for the rest of the world. At this moment, the world is paying attention to the canary because it is clearly suffering, although it is not dead yet. It seems to be a reasonable assumption that global attention will shift away from the Arctic as climate change impacts will be felt more acutely elsewhere, in particular in more densely populated areas of highly developed nations. Attention might return to the Arctic in the future if large scale events, such as a rapid melting of the Greenland ice sheet, will pose more imminent threats. The interests of the international legal community are fluctuating, which is a natural phenomenon as international law reacts to challenges and social needs. The current interest of international lawyers in the Arctic will not be permanent. Climate change means that the Arctic ocean is becoming more and more like the North Atlantic. Similarly, international Arctic law is becoming more codified, transitioning from soft to hard law (cf. Koivurova, 2014), thereby becoming more like international law elsewhere. The cooperation in the Arctic Council can be a model for regional cooperation elsewhere, but Arctic Law is, at this moment, in a hinge position, connecting soft and hard law, cooperation and disagreements, transitioning from an emerging field of international law to a more regular form of regional international law. The EU's new policy document highlights the opportunities that are inherent in this moment of opportunity to let cooperation based on international law prevail over conflict or inaction.

References

1. European Union [Commission] (2008). Communication from the Commission to the European Parliament and the Council, The European Union and the Arctic Region, 20 November 2008, COM(2008) 763 final.
2. European Union [Council of the European Union] (2014). Conclusions on developing a European Union Policy towards the Arctic Region, 12 May 2014, https://www.consilium.europa.eu/media/28342/142554.pdf.
3. European Union [Council of the European Union] (2016). Conclusions on the Arctic, 20 June 2016, para. 2, https://data.consilium.europa.eu/doc/document/ST-10400-2016-INIT/en/pdf.
4. European Union [European Commission & High Representative of the Union on Foreign Policy and Security Policy] (2016a). Joint Communication to the European Parliament and the Council: An integrated European Union Policy for the Arctic, 27 April 2016, JOIN(2016) 21 final, https://eeas.europa.eu/archives/docs/arctic_region/docs/160427_joint-communication-an-integrated-european-union-policy-for-the-arctic_en.pdf.
5. European Union [European Commission & High Representative of the European Union for Foreign Affairs and Security Policy] (2012). Joint Communication to the European Parliament and the Council, Developing a European Union Policy towards the Arctic Region: progress since 2008 and next steps. 26 June 2012, JOIN(2012) 19 final.
6. European Union [European Commission & High Representative of the Union for Foreign Affairs and Security Policy] (2021). Joint Communication to the European Parliament, the Council, the European Economic and Social Committee and the Committee of the Regions – A stronger EU engagement for a peaceful, sustainable and prosperous Arctic, 13 October 2021, JOIN(2021) 27, https://eeas.europa.eu/sites/default/files/2_en_act_part1_v7.pdf.

7. European Union [European Parliament] (2011). Resolution on a sustainable EU policy for the High North, 20 January 2011, Doc P7_TA (2011) 0024.
8. European Union [European Commission] (2021a). Questions and answers on the EU's Arctic Strategy. 13 October 2021, https://ec.europa.eu/commission/presscorner/detail/en/qanda_21_5164.
9. Koivurova, T. (2014). Increasing Relevance of Treaties: The Case of the Arctic. AJIL Unbound, 108, 52-56. doi:10.1017/S2398772300001847, https://www.cambridge.org/core/journals/american-journal-of-international-law/article/increasing-relevance-of-treaties-the-case-of-the-arctic/CE72839C61E509A6CF18931559658048.
10. Lowen, M. (2021). Pope urges 'radical' climate response in exclusive BBC message. BBC. 29 October 2021, https://www.bbc.com/news/world-europe-59075041.

CONCLUSIONS AND OUTLOOK
Ayonghe Akonwi Nebasifu

This book came about as an attempt to create and intensify awareness of the Arctic within the scope of Arctic Law and Arctic Governance. Indeed, an attempt, when we consider just how inexhaustive there are practical realities and issues of interest pertaining to securitization of the Arctic, environmental protection, questions of indigenous rights, and the jurisdiction of States when it comes to the use and management of natural resources in both terrestrial and marine environments. This list goes on, which cannot be entirely covered in this book based on its format requirements. What however looks obvious, which must be taken seriously, is the complex nature of the Arctic – a region that is warming three times faster than elsewhere on the planet, and yet, more and more non-Arctic actors want to be involved in this fragile region and in decision-making about the Arctic, be it over technology, maritime activities, oil and gas exploration, tourism, commercial fishing, energy, and so on.

Concerns at large in the Arctic are often shared across the region's communities, its numerous stakeholders, indigenous groups, and local residents. For example, when we think of the region's colonial legacies, environmental pollution, suicides, conflict over military activities, and evidently climate change. Efforts to protect the Arctic's natural environment are not new, and neither it is, when it comes to cooperation, both among Arctic actors and non-Arctic actors. In fact, as was mentioned in this book's foreword chapter, a thaw had already begun in the international relations between East and West earlier on in 1989, with suggestions to have a conference to address the status quo of environmental protection in the Arctic. Following dialogues in the same year, in Rovaniemi, the Arctic Environmental Protection Strategy (AEPS) was introduced. And in 1996, with the creation of the Arctic Council (AC), by eight Arctic States, the AC remains a fundamental forum for cross-border cooperation on Arctic Governance. However, as ongoing challenges in the Arctic continue to affect various stakeholders, communities in the Arctic, as well as, actors who tend to be involved in the Arctic even when they are far away in other parts of the world, there is, as a necessity, a need to increase awareness of the Arctic which is home to valuable species, millions of people, and in particular, the indigenous Sámi, Inuit, and other groups that have for several decades inhabited this region.

To modestly draw attention to the ongoing concerns in the region, a number of authors came together with a collection of chapters in this book, to address some of the threats to the Arctic environment from the stance of Arctic Law and Arctic Governance, and how both concepts could better function to address the current needs in the Arctic region. The authors here, all share common thoughts about the problems at hand with the spirit to keep the academic community alive. It seems, reading by their essays, it is clear to me that complex problems largely require diverse and holistic solutions, though with some exceptions. With a growing global interest in the Arctic today among non-Arctic actors who want to be inclusive of decisions made about the Arctic, the authors agree, there is need for appropriate steps towards cooperation as well as clarity in the law. In this conclusion, I will first of all draw on some of the key contributions from authors in this book to summarise and provide an outlook on some of the pertinent problems in the Arctic. For example, ranging from vessel-source pollution and competing interests between Flag states and Coastal tates, questions over the legality of foreign military activities in the Exclusive Economic Zone (EEZ), China's role in the securitization of the Arctic, disaster impact on the transfer of technology within international economic law, the nexus between space operations and the Arctic natural environment, to the procedures of the European Union (EU) towards banning oil and gas exploration. Secondly, I will reflect in each of the above problems, what suggestions could be followed. My chapter will then conclude with what these reflections, or proposals per se, imply for the future direction of Arctic Law and Arctic Governance.

Rigidity, inexplicitness, or slow reactions in international law? The need for a globalized consensus against marine pollution in the Arctic

Over the recent decade, the Arctic Ocean has gained significant global attention, with regards to the varied interests flag states and coastal states share, their role, responsibility, and jurisdiction, with respect to vessel-source pollution, competition over the Ocean's resources, and the legal norms that exist to protect the Arctic Marine environment and wellbeing of the local residents. Many treaties exist within international law to protect the marine environment, but they often appear as puzzles that need to be fit together, reinforced, and given more clarity to meet up with today's challenges facing the Arctic's natural environment. This habitually requires legal action between flag stages and coastal states in terms of their capacity to protect the marine environment. Article 56 of the United Nations Convention on the Law of the Sea (UNCLOS) recognizes the legal capacity for flag states (e.g. Canada) to protect the marine environment within their internal waters. Also, by Article 234 of UNCLOS, flag states have responsibility for vessel-source pollution in areas beyond national jurisdiction. For instance, the high seas' Central Arctic Ocean. There is however no single Arctic treaty on this matter, but additional elements to the provisions of UNCLOS do exist, among other frameworks (customary international laws and international treaties) that regulate the Arctic Ocean such as the International Law of the Seas developed through the 2008 Ilulissat Declaration. Two other legal frameworks, the International Convention for the Safety of Life at Sea (SOLAS) and the International Convention for the Prevention of Pollution from Ships (MARPOL) providing rules for protecting the safety of vessels and people in the seas have been adopted by the International Maritime Organization (IMO). SOLAS and MARPOL however do not provide for a regional seas agreement for regulating protection of the Arctic marine environment.

Although IMO regulates measures for ships to comply with the switch to low-sulphur content fuels, the Paris agreement does not cover for regulating the shipping industry. But also, there are concerns about the increase in transport costs when transitioning to cleaner sources of fuel which then results in concerns over food security as seen in the Greenland to Denmark case. Many ships are registered in countries that are far from where they operate and there are also significant differences in technological use systems between flag states when compared to the global technological system. This brings about technically limited ability for flag states to ensure that registered ships in their country comply with international standards. In the cargo shipping sector, it is also hard for Port State Control (PSC) to ensure compliance to international standards when we think of the very short turnaround times in ports and the risk of profit loss which triggers the unattractiveness of certain ports to shipping companies.

What then can be done to promote a globalized effort and consensus against vessel-source pollution in the Arctic? The AC provides a suitable forum for the entire Arctic region and its eight Member States as well as non-Arctic actors who also contribute to Arctic Governance as Observers to the AC. In principle, this also gives an opportunity for constructive discussions towards a globalized consensus to protect the Arctic marine environment. While there exist varied opinions about climate change, members of AC do share a common consensus that certain challenges have to be addressed for the entire Arctic region. Scientific research on the Arctic Ocean also offers a gate way to mobilizing global efforts against marine pollution in the context of cross-border cooperation between states with different political trajectories (Berkman, 2020). It will also be advantageous protecting the Arctic Ocean if measures of designating certain areas in the Arctic Ocean as Particularly Sensitive Sea Area in response to unregulated fishing and other threats from shipping to the sea. Already, a mandatory route for ships travelling through deeper waters of the Wadden Sea in the North Sea has been developed under Associated Protective Measures (APM). Similarly, in the Baltic Sea, there exist traffic schemes to ensure that ships travelling to one direction follow the same route, distinct from the route used by ships travelling the opposite direction. This is helping to reduce accidents of ship collision and oil spills in the ocean.

Unclarity in the legal nature of military exercises in the Exclusive Economic Zones (EEZ) - towards appropriate standardization and prior notification systems at sea

In 1982, EEZs were introduced applicable to waters located up to 200 nautical miles from baselines. Within this parameter, lies the sovereign right for coastal states to enjoy the economic potential of natural resources as well as exercise their jurisdiction over activities to preserve the marine environment. However, the legality of EEZs are very much unclear as to how foreign military activities can be treated. While some coastal states do use the EEZ of other states, there are disputes concerning questions over the legality of this practice. We have seen the example of military activities performed in August 2020, in the Bering Sea by the Russian Federation under the Ocean Shield 2020 Operations, where in US-flagged fishing vessels were directed away from the US EEZ on the pretext of concerns linked to the safety associated with missile lunches. This incident compromised not only the safety navigation of US-flagged fishing vessels but also the freedom of fishing. Under UNCLOS, the peaceful use of the seas is an essential principle, but in reality, it is rather hard to define what aspect of military exercises and manoeuvres in the seas can be categorized as peaceful. UNCLOS however specifies that a military activity may be prohibited if is an act of aggression. One can also argue that, USA is not a contracting party to UNCLOS yet its EEZ extends 200 nautical miles from baseline – which makes its hard to have an accurate interpretation or judgement of the Ocean Shield 2020 Operations incident. Even when looking into the 1990 US/USSR Agreement, the way of simply exchanging notes after signing, without any further steps to incorporate the agreement into domestic legislation also calls into question the nature of the 2020 incident. This agreement even till today, remains to be incorporated into domestic legislation.

One of the causes of this incident was attributed to the unclear nature of legal procedures between military activity and commercial fishing – combined with inadequate advanced notice on military exercises which all led to limiting the freedom of US fishing vessels with regard to navigation and fishing. It should be noted here that coastal states do not have absolute control over all uses of the EEZ, when taking into consideration Article 56 of UNCLOS which outlines the sovereign rights of coastal states in a non-exhaustive and yet non-precise manner (Beckman & Davenport, 2012). As divergent views continue to exist about coastal states and their rights and jurisdiction over military activities in the EEZ, a few suggestions must be made for better standardization and prior notification in communication systems at sea which could bring about suitable options for the co-existence of military and economic activities at sea. Currently, there is a World-Wide Navigational Warning Service (WWNWS) jointly established by IMO and the International Hydrographic Organization (IHO) in 1979, to ensure efficiency in coordinating navigational warning through standardization – content and formats of messages, and zoning of the seas (Soluri, 1998). This is being reinforced by SOLAS through the obligation for all ships to be properly equipped with broadcasting systems for navigational warnings as SafetyNET. However, Russia and USA each use varied communication channels for warning systems which has the tendency to jeopardize the efficiency of WWNWS. The effectiveness of maritime EEZs will therefore rest on better harmonization and standardization of notification and communication channels, inclusive of international efforts to ensure detailed instructions for prior notification when carrying out foreign military activities within EEZs. The Indian and Pakistan case of adopting a bilateral agreement on advanced notice (India-Pakistan Agreement, 1991) is a good example we can learn from.

CONCLUSIONS AND OUTLOOK 179

China's role in Arctic securitization: towards a better analysis of constructs on existential threats in the Arctic?

The Arctic White Paper, China's Arctic Policy published in 2018 indicating China's mission to promote peace in the Arctic, share interest on securing concerns over military activities, energy, navigation, and resources. In the 2020 Climate Ambition Summit, President Xi Jinping made mention of China's mission to achieve carbon neutrality before 2060. Chapter four in this book has taken a further step to contextualize China's role in the securitization of the Arctic as an actor that uses climate change as an incentive to justify its legitimacy of participating in the Arctic including other affairs as energy and navigation. This is not surprising. When we look at the 2015 National Assessment Report on Climate Change of the Chinese Ministry of Science and Technology, it articulates that climate change relates to China's security within the areas of the economy, energy, ecology, and food. This securitization, as has been argued by the authors, is triggered by benefits and threats, with it being more of the benefits. Indeed, the recent 21st century fundamental discourse on climate change in the Arctic has been the rapid melting of sea ice and the opening of the Northern sea route. As China pursues its mission of transitioning to carbon neutrality, the country also experiences a rapid growing demand in domestic energy. As the Arctic's energy sources increasingly become of global interest, China is opting towards economic benefits of the Arctic shipping routes and diversify the security threats it faces in traditional maritime routes in the Pacific and Indo-Pacific regions that are prone to pirate attacks, higher cost of navigation, and longer navigational distances. China, seeking active role in making decisions about the Arctic will definitely secure its mission towards cleaner energy. Arctic shipping routes are also stable socio-politically and will enable China gain critical access to Arctic natural resources. Along the lines of understanding how various actors (securitizing and functional) develop constructs of securitization offers suitable knowledge about existential threats to Arctic security and what implications such constructs provide for enhancing cooperation in Arctic Governance and Securitization.

Fragmented international disaster laws: Towards better knowledge, evidence, and cooperation on space-based technological transfer

As any other region in the world, the Arctic is equally prone to all kinds of disasters, both on land and sea. This has several economic consequences on Arctic states, which is why space technology is becoming an essential tool for monitoring disasters. But in terms of knowledge, what sought of elements come into play concerning the transfer of space-based technologies in the context of international disaster law? Following the occurrence of a hydrometeorological disaster, the damage being inflicted may require the importation of several goods and services, creation of debt, some governments borrow to finance recovery. The World Trade Organization (WTO) has taken a step to establish a report on the impact of natural disasters on trade and what kind of legal measures governments can take to respond (WTO, 2020). The World Intellectual Property Organization (WIPO) also defines technology transfer a series of processes that include sharing knowledge, skills, ideas, and technology with another individual or institution. This technology can be in several forms as in designs, patents, trademarks, machinery, written documents and so on (WIPO, 2011). Disasters could trigger delays in the transfer of technological equipment, increase costs in custom clearances, to even affecting global production and supply networks.

However, international disaster laws are themselves quite fragmented, with some laws focusing on disaster and others on technology transfer. Finding a common indication of international flows of technology in international disaster law is rather hard. For instance, the Sendai Framework on Disaster Risk Reduction 2015-2030 adopted during the 2015 UN World Conference on Disaster Risk Reduction outlines certain provisions on technology transfer and shares resilience strategies, but lacks any reference on trade policy in disaster preparedness. Also, when it comes to the transfer of sensitive or codified technological data, the benefit of speedy disaster response based on sharing or exchange risk being hampered. Cooperation in the use of satellite data for disaster relief and risk-management would do much to reveal knowledge on what fragmental pieces to consider in the place of international disaster law along with better alternatives for disaster-risk management. Data from earth observation satellites do offer vital information to predict disasters, monitor pollution, and changes in the environment. Already, some examples show ongoing efforts towards space-based technological transfer at the level of state cooperation, which I believe are pieces we can learn from to bring about the knowledge, evidence, and cooperation needed in the transfer of space-based technology. The Council of the European Union concluded in 2019 its statement on space solutions for a sustainable Arctic stating the potential for satellite communications and navigation, earth observation and space weather observation, to addressing challenges in the Arctic region. Within the Arctic Council, a Task Force on Improved Connectivity in the Arctic was created in 2017 with its goal to overview best practices for commercial opportunities and technological solutions in the Arctic. This has gone a long way to gather representatives of various business entities, stakeholders, authorities, and organizations to engage with the telecommunication sector and make use of space-based technologies. In 2021, Swedish space systems providers ESA and OHB Sweden, signed a contract to contract a prototype satellite by 2024 that would offer climatic data on the Arctic necessary for disaster management.

Impacts of space operations: Towards reduced-risk of human casualties
Several rocket launch sites locate north of the Arctic Circle, from the Svalbard Rocket Range in Ny-Ålesund, Andøya Space Center in Andenes, Norway, Esrange near Kiruna, Sweden, to Russia's Plesetsk Cosmodrome in Arkhangelsk oblast. Rocket returning to earth as a planned exercise or for technical failures, and the rocket fuel and debris from launch stages have devastating impacts on the natural

environment, wildlife, and even the livelihoods of indigenous people in the Arctic region. For instance, the case of rocket stages launched in North Russia that came down in Baffin Bay, a homeland to the Inuit, raising legal and health concerns. To therefore adopt suitable measures for reducing the risks of human casualties from rocket launch sites, rules governing space operations will need to go beyond space law to include norms about the Arctic's natural environment. Also, with the increasing use of reusable launch stages that are more profiting and less costly, there is risk that many more of such stages will be created in the Arctic which raises concerns of security. A number of legal instruments already exist with ideas linked to indigenous and environmental human rights which can be incorporated into Space Law. For instance: the European Convention on Human Rights (ECHR) which recognizes the right to a healthy environment and obliges all parties to this convention to stay away from activities that endanger human health; the 2007 UN Declaration on the Rights of Indigenous Peoples which indicates the right of indigenous peoples to free, prior and informed consent; and the ILO Convention 169 which develop customary international law. Conducting cross-border environmental impact assessments (EIAs) would be another important step to protect the rights of indigenous communities and local residents affected by rocket launches, and exchange environmental information vital to reduce any risk of human casualties. Modern space law must therefore have an environmental dimension not limited only to treaties and regulatory efforts. As there is an increasing need for lawyers to look beyond their specialties into other disciplines of law in order to better deal with today's environmental problems, so too, it would be useful, if practitioners of Space Law were to broaden their view beyond the usual norms in international space law and to consider indigenous, human, and environmental rights.

Oil and gas exploration: Towards a multilateral legal obligation?
The last concern I had like to address is that of oil and gas exploration. It is not new to hear that the extraction of hydrocarbon contributes significantly to climate change in the Arctic and elsewhere around the world. But there has not yet been a legally binding multilateral obligation within the European Union (EU) to stop any further hydrocarbon reserve development. As concerns the Arctic, we have seen Russia's intension to build its economy through future exportation of hydrocarbons from the Arctic, meanwhile Norway is already decarbonizing its economy, although the country concurrently exports hydrocarbons. Existing legalities at the EU level does indicate some efforts towards decarbonization. For instance, when we look at the EU's 2016 Arctic policy document focusing on climate change and sustainable development. The EU's 2021 updated Arctic Policy document, communicated just before the start of COP26, goes on to highlight the need for a stronger EU engagement with regards to a peaceful, sustainable, and prosperous Arctic. The 2021 document stresses the EU's commitment to ensure that oil, coal, and gas stay in the ground, while also calling for an international binding legal obligation. Concretizing these efforts will require not just clarifying already existing legal questions on climate change, but also establishing closer relations and dialogue with local stakeholders and indigenous communities in the Arctic.

Overarchingly, what seems connected in all the concerns discussed in this book, is that of fragmentation in international law. As the challenges of climate change around the world continue to fluctuate, transition, and display in complex ways, many of the international legal instruments and their provisions will require clarifications. So too, as there is increasing international interest in the Arctic, its natural resources, and people, which explains the complexity of the Arctic, it will benefit Arctic Governance, inducing some legal elements of international law into Arctic Law so to include other dimensions (customary law, environmental law, indigenous rights etc.) capable of addressing today's climate change crisis. The Arctic Council which stands at one of the Arctic region's top-level forum for cross-border cooperation between eight Member States, can be not only a model for regional cooperation elsewhere, but for experimenting options for which effective international legalities on securitization applied somewhere else in the world can be encouraged within Arctic Law so to strengthening Arctic Governance.

References
1. Beckman, R. & Davenport, T. (2012). The EEZ Regime: Reflections After 30 Years. In Proceedings from the 2012 LOSI-KIOST Conference on Securing the Ocean for the Next Generation. Available at: https://www.law.berkeley.edu/files/Beckman-Davenport-final.pdf.
2. Berkman, Paul Arthur (2020). "Polar science diplomacy", in: Scott, Karen N. & Vander Zwaag, David L. (eds.), Research Handbook on Polar Law, Cheltenham: Edward Elgar, pp. 105-123.
3. India-Pakistan Agreement (1991). Agreement on Advance Notice on Military Exercises, Manoeuvres and Troop Movements, adopted 6 April 1991. https://treaties.un.org/doc/publication/unts/volume%201843/volume-1843-i-31420-english.pdf
4. Soluri, E. A. (1998). Promulgation of Navigational Warnings under the Global Maritime Distress and Safety System. International Hydrographic Review, LXXV(2), 15-25.
5. WIPO [World Intellectual Property Organization] (2011, April 13). Transfer of Technology. Standing Committee on the Law of Patents, SCP/14/4 REV. http://www.wipo.int/edocs/mdocs/scp/en/scp_16/scp_14_4_rev.pdf.
6. WTO (2020). Research on natural disasters and trade. https://www.wto.org/english/tratop_e/devel_e/a4t_e/researchnaturdisaster_e.htm.

EPILOGUE
Stefan Kirchner

Climate change impacts the Arctic and the people who live there. The perception of the Arctic becoming more accessible due to climate change – although melting permafrost actually affects transport infrastructure negatively – leads to an increasing interest in the Arctic. From different vantage points, different aspects of the Arctic appear more or less important. For the millions of people who live in the Arctic, including indigenous peoples who can trace their ancestors' histories in the region back thousands of years, the Arctic is home and the natural environment of the Arctic is a source of more than just food but at the heart of local cultures. Seen from the outside, different ideas about the Arctic can be identified. The Arctic is seen by at times as an exotic location, while its environment is also vulnerable and in need of protection. But the Arctic is also perceived as a place of economic opportunities. The realization of economic opportunities in the thinly populated region that offers limited economic opportunities and where sustainable development remains a challenge often involves methods that are harmful for the natural environment on which all Arctic residents depend. This includes the extraction of hydrocarbons – oil, gas and coal – from the Arctic. The burning of these fossil fuels in turn worsens climate change and its negative impacts in the Arctic and around the world. Differing visions of the Arctic and different approaches to the Arctic also increase the relevance of discussions concerning the use of technologies for different purposes in the Arctic as well as about hard security questions. While the protection of the natural environment and the sustainable development of the Arctic region, as well as climate change, have long been key concerns in Arctic governance, the Arctic Council has refrained from dealing with hard security issues since its inception. Questions concerning security and safety and the use of different technologies for different purposes, often with major impacts on the natural environment, from mining and the construction of infrastructure to geoengineering and operations at sea and in outer space, these issues are likely to remain relevant for the foreseeable future. The texts collected in this anthology provide some food for thought and are meant to whet the reader's appetite for more information. The governance of the Arctic, balancing different rights and interests, involving not only states but also non-state actors and especially local stakeholders, including indigenous peoples, remains a work in progress. Almost all parts of the Arctic have experienced often painful colonial histories and although there is still significant room for improvement when it comes to respecting the rights of the indigenous peoples of the Arctic, contemporary Arctic law has a place for indigenous peoples. Future decisions about the governance will have to take in account the views, needs, interests and rights of the people who live in the Arctic. Newly emerging challenges will lead to difficult questions, but the international legal community of the Arctic, the actors in Arctic governance, have the benefit of a young but already well-established governance framework, based on international law, that will facilitate the search for answers. This search will benefit from the open exchange of ideas and views. The Arctic has a chance to become a role model for international cooperation if the willingness to listen to each other despite major differences is maintained. Hopefully, this book will have made a small contribution to keeping this spirit alive.

INDEX

A

Arctic ... 1, 2, 4, 5, 6, 1, 2, 4, 8, 9, 10, 11, 12, 13, 14, 15, 16, 20, 21, 22, 23, 24, 25, 26, 27, 29, 30, 31, 32, 33, 34, 36, 49, 51, 53, 57, 58, 59, 60, 61, 62, 63, 64, 65, 67, 68, 69, 70, 71, 72, 73, 74, 75, 76, 77, 78, 79, 80, 81, 82, 83, 84, 85, 86, 87, 88, 89, 90, 91, 92, 93, 94, 95, 96, 97, 98, 99, 100, 101, 102, 103, 104, 105, 106, 107, 108, 109, 110, 111, 112, 113, 114, 115, 116, 118, 130, 131, 132, 133, 134, 136, 137, 139, 140, 141, 142, 143, 144, 145, 149, 150, 156, 160, 162, 163, 165, 166, 168, 169, 171, 172, 173, 174, 175, 176, 179, 180, 181, 183, 185

Arctic Circle 70, 97, 101, 105, 140, 181

Arctic Council 1, 2, 8, 23, 24, 27, 63, 87, 89, 95, 103, 131, 133, 170, 173, 181, 183, 185

Arctic governance. 1, 4, 1, 8, 33, 59, 72, 185

Arctic hydrocarbon development 11, 166

Arctic Ocean. 1, 8, 9, 13, 14, 15, 20, 23, 24, 25, 26, 27, 49, 70, 142, 175, 176

Arctic policy 9, 11, 80, 165, 168, 183

Arctic security.. 59, 63, 93, 98, 106, 179

Arctic shipping ... 13, 24, 58, 63, 65, 74, 92, 112, 179

Arctic White Paper... 58, 70, 71, 77, 82, 87, 179

B

Baltic Sea 15, 23, 26, 176

Bering Sea 9, 33, 34, 35, 36, 39, 46, 48, 50, 51, 53, 54, 177

C

Carbon neutrality 73, 80, 84, 102, 179

Cargo shipping sector............ 22, 176

China 6, 9, 57, 58, 59, 60, 61, 63, 64, 65, 66, 67, 68, 69, 70, 71, 72, 73, 74, 75, 76, 77, 78, 79, 80, 81, 82, 83, 84, 85, 86, 88, 89, 90, 91, 92, 93, 94, 95, 96, 97, 98, 99, 100, 101, 102, 103, 104, 105, 106, 107, 108, 109, 110, 111, 112, 113, 114, 169, 174, 179

Climate change. 1, 2, 5, 4, 9, 11, 13, 16, 18, 20, 24, 25, 32, 33, 57, 58, 59, 60, 61, 63, 65, 66, 67, 68, 69, 70, 71, 72, 73, 84, 85, 86, 89, 95, 96, 103, 107, 141, 156, 158, 165, 166, 168, 169, 173, 176, 179, 183, 185

Coal 11, 73, 81, 83, 165, 167, 168, 169, 183, 185

Coastal states 8, 13, 15, 23, 26, 175, 177, 178
Community 2, 10, 25, 67, 117, 143, 146, 151, 152, 155, 156, 159, 170, 174, 186
Copenhagen School of Securitization 58, 68

D

Disaster management. 127, 132, 181
Disaster preparedness..........121, 180
Disasters......10, 115, 116, 117, 118, 119, 124, 126, 127, 129, 130, 132, 135, 137, 138, 180, 181, 184

E

Economic opportunities 59, 185
Energy Security ..58, 59, 60, 67, 72, 73, 74, 75, 76, 77, 78, 79, 80, 81, 83, 85, 90, 94, 102, 110, 112, 113, 114, 165
Environment 1, 2, 1, 2, 7, 8, 13, 15, 20, 23, 24, 25, 26, 34, 45, 58, 69, 70, 71, 78, 84, 90, 100, 102, 107, 115, 139, 140, 141, 143, 144, 145, 146, 147, 148, 149, 150, 151, 152, 153, 154, 155, 158, 168, 169, 173, 174, 175, 176, 177, 181, 182, 185
Environmental protection.. ....8, 10, 15, 139, 165, 173
European Green Deal 165
European Union....... 11, 30, 93, 100, 125, 131, 134, 135, 140, 147, 163, 165, 166, 167, 168, 171, 172, 174, 181, 183
Exclusive Economic Zone........ 9, 14, 33, 50, 51, 52, 53, 174, 177
Exploration 9, 11, 58, 76, 77, 83, 97, 127, 129, 165, 167, 173, 174, 183
Extraction ...2, 11, 65, 93, 153, 166, 168, 169, 183, 185

G

Gas... 11, 28, 63, 72, 73, 74, 75, 77, 91, 93, 95, 96, 97, 98, 99, 101, 107, 109, 112, 165, 167, 168, 169, 173, 174, 183, 185
Greenhouse Gas emissions... 13, 16, 17, 18, 19

H

Human rights 2, 4, 6, 2, 10, 78, 139, 145, 146, 147, 150, 152, 155, 157, 158, 182
Hydrocarbons..........11, 74, 165, 166, 168, 169, 183, 185

I

IMO 13, 15, 16, 17, 18, 19, 20, 24, 28, 30, 45, 46, 51, 156, 175, 178
Indigenous peoples.. ....2, 23, 139, 142, 144, 145, 151, 152, 154, 168, 182, 185
Indigenous rights 139, 150, 159, 168, 173, 183
Infrastructure.... 116, 124, 142, 185

INDEX

International cooperation 1, 6, 24, 72, 77, 91, 121, 127, 128, 129, 186
International disaster law ... 10, 115, 120, 126, 180
International economic law 10, 115, 120, 132, 174
International law of the Sea 8, 9, 15, 33, 34, 175
Inuit 142, 143, 144, 145, 174, 182

L

Local cultures 185

M

Marine pollution 13, 17, 175, 176
Maritime routes 179
Military activities 9, 33, 34, 35, 36, 39, 40, 41, 42, 43, 44, 45, 46, 47, 48, 173, 174, 177, 178, 179
Military threats 2, 61, 64

N

National security 2, 4, 9, 57, 58, 59, 60, 63, 65, 66, 68, 70, 72, 74, 76, 77, 83, 86, 92, 95, 110, 112, 113
Natural environment ... 1, 2, 14, 139, 140, 141, 143, 144, 145, 156, 169, 173, 174, 175, 182, 185
Natural hazards 3, 124, 131, 133
North Sea 26, 176
Northern sea route 179

O

Oil 11, 15, 25, 61, 63, 72, 73, 74, 75, 93, 95, 96, 97, 98, 101, 107, 165, 167, 168, 169, 173, 174, 177, 183, 185

P

Pandemic 93, 165
Paris agreement 168, 175
Permafrost 141, 185
Pollution 1, 8, 13, 15, 21, 31, 131, 139, 140, 148, 156, 173, 174, 175, 176, 181

R

Renewable energies 165
Russia 36, 38, 39, 49, 50, 51, 52, 53, 54, 55, 74, 75, 80, 93, 99, 102, 103, 105, 106, 110, 140, 142, 145, 166, 169, 178, 181, 183

S

Safety 9, 15, 17, 21, 23, 25, 33, 34, 37, 38, 43, 45, 46, 47, 48, 49, 69, 175, 177, 185
Sámi 143, 144, 145, 168, 174
Satellites .. 127, 131, 139, 140, 144, 181
Securitization of the Arctic .. 58, 59, 60, 64, 73, 86, 173, 174, 179
Security 2, 1, 2, 3, 4, 5, 6, 8, 9, 10, 11, 12, 20, 23, 33, 34, 44, 46, 49, 57, 58, 59, 60, 61, 62, 63, 64, 65, 66, 68, 69, 70, 71, 72, 73, 74, 75, 76, 77, 78, 79, 80,

81, 83, 84, 85, 86, 89, 90, 92, 94, 95, 96, 97, 98, 101, 102, 103, 106, 108, 109, 110, 111, 112, 113, 131, 139, 143, 144, 156, 165, 176, 179, 182, 185
Space 2, 10, 58, 66, 84, 85, 115, 116, 118, 126, 127, 128, 129, 130, 131, 132, 134, 135, 136, 137, 138, 139, 140, 143, 144, 145, 149, 154, 155, 157, 158, 159, 162, 164, 174, 180, 181, 182, 186
Space Law ... 5, 138, 144, 145, 161, 162, 164, 182
Space technologies 10
Space-based 10, 115, 116, 118, 126, 127, 129, 130, 131, 132, 180, 181
Stakeholders. 10, 63, 130, 131, 132, 168, 173, 181, 183, 186
Sustainable development 1, 2, 24, 134, 144, 146, 165, 183, 185

T

Technological action 5, 7

Technological solutions 21, 131, 181
Technology 2, 1, 2, 5, 6, 7, 8, 10, 12, 18, 104, 115, 116, 118, 119, 120, 121, 122, 123, 124, 126, 127, 128, 129, 131, 132, 134, 135, 137, 138, 154, 173, 174, 180
Technology transfer 10, 18, 115, 118, 120, 121, 122, 123, 124, 126, 127, 128, 129, 131, 132, 133, 135, 180
Treaty 15, 19, 43, 54, 134, 166, 175

U

United Nations 14, 16, 27, 29, 32, 35, 39, 41, 51, 53, 55, 68, 117, 118, 127, 129, 136, 137, 142, 156, 158, 163, 164, 167, 175
United States of America 4, 56, 177, 178

W

Wadden Sea 26, 176

Stefan Kirchner (Ed.)
Governing the Crisis: Law, Human Rights and COVID-19
Governing the Crisis: Law, Human Rights and COVID-19 is a collection of essays by an interdisciplinary group of experts from around the world who look at different human rights issues which have emerged as relevant during the COVID-19 pandemic. The topics cover a range of issues in different countries, for example, tracing apps, digitalization, privacy, priority setting in health care, refugees, cruise ships or risks faced by children. Other chapters investigate the specific government responses in a number of countries. In addition, topics of wider legal interest are investigated, such as the role of constitutional courts, federalism and the concept of the state of emergency.
2021, 298 S., 44,90 EUR, br., ISBN 978-3-643-91351-7

Timo Koivurova; Henrik Ringbom; Pirjo Kleemola-Juntunen; Stefan Kirchner
The Baltic Sea and the Law of the Sea – Finnish Perspectives
The Baltic Sea is unique with regard to its geography, climate and environment. Its uniqueness is also reflected in policy and governance. The book examines the regulation of the Baltic Sea from different perspectives, including navigation, the protection of the marine environment, fisheries, marine scientific research and future challenges for the law of the sea in the Baltic Sea. The book thus also represents a maritime case study of how international, European and national laws interact in the Baltic Sea Region.
2019, 130 S., 29,90 EUR, br., ISBN 978-3-643-80292-7

LIT Verlag Berlin – Münster – Wien – Zürich – London
Auslieferung Deutschland / Österreich / Schweiz: siehe Impressumsseite